China's Food

中國食物

China's Food

A

Photographic

Journey

by

Reinhart

Wolf

Text

by

Lionel

Tiger

中國食物

Recipes by

Eileen Yin-Fei Lo

Published by Friendly Press, Inc., 401 Park Avenue South,
New York City, NY 10016, United States of America.
Set in Goudy Old Style type.
Designed by Lazin & Katalan.
Printed in Italy by Arnoldo Mondadori Editore Verona.

Some photographs in this book were taken with a Sinar 8 x 10
camera, some with a Hasselblad 2½ x 2¼, and some with a
Nikon 35mm. The film used was Ektachrome daylight. Most
were taken with available daylight. In some still lifes, electronic
flash was used.

Library of Congress Cataloging in Publication Data

Tiger, Lionel, 1937–
China's food.

1. Cookery, Chinese. 2. Food habits—China. 3. China—
Description and travel—1976–   . I. Wolf, Reinhart,
1930–   . II. Title.
TX724.5.C5T53 1985 641.3'0951 85-70860
ISBN 0-914919-02-4

Acknowledgments

This was a complex project made possible only by the skillful cooperation and counsel of many people. We are deeply grateful to everyone of the China International Travel Service who handled the countless details of the voyage with aplomb and decency. The quality of their management is reflected in the fact that during a three-month period up to a half dozen people and dozens of containers of valuable and fragile equipment were moved on a daily basis without a single loss, or damage.

We thank Gisela Lübbe-Zimmermann for her help with the photographs accompanying the recipes. We are also grateful to Ikarus Travel.

This is our happy opportunity to thank the people with whom we worked at Friendly Press. Their graceful but brisk professionalism was as reassuring when we were far away in China as their warmth and humor were a pleasure in New York. Liv Reed and Maggie Groening were especially buoyant. We want in particular to record our appreciation for the energy and creativity of Peggy Flaum, Marty Goldstein, and Stuart Waldman.

R.W.
L.T.

Preface

A note is in order about the two people principally involved in preparing this book. Reinhart Wolf has been celebrated internationally as a photographer of people, things, buildings, and food. He has a weekly feature in *Stern* magazine and has shown his work in galleries in Europe, North America, and Asia. His book *New York* is widely admired for its striking photographs of the rooftops of the city's characteristic sky-scrapers, providing a fresh look at the force and beauty of things normally taken for granted. He has published *Castles in Spain,* as well as two cookbooks in Germany, where he has taught photography. He heads a major photographic studio in Hamburg and receives commissions from throughout Europe.

I am an anthropologist who has long been interested in the underlying biology of human behavior, and how our evolution as a species affects the way we organize our contemporary communities: how a four- or five-million-year-old highly intelligent primate lives in a very new—just two hundred years old—industrial system. Insofar as anthropology is the science of human culture, it is quite in order to study how people have fun and games, and what these mean to their lives in general. And while food is, of course, about survival first, most humans stubbornly insist on having fun where food is concerned, and I have found myself fascinated by this phenomenon. And since food habits and preferences have a real impact on health, I have also been interested in how different societies adjust their diets to accommodate both the taste preferences we formed during our evolution and the foods that are available to us today. For example, neat sugar did not exist in the world before its cultivation relatively recently as sugarcane. But the human species in general has a "sweet tooth," which probably evolved to encourage us to eat the fruits and vegetables we need. To get a bit of sweetness, we ate a lot of apple or carrot. Even as late as the Renaissance, straight sugar was a great luxury. Indeed, when we learned how to cultivate sugar the demand for it became so great and so uncontrollable that it was in large part responsible for the maintenance of the ghastly system of slavery.

I must also report by way of confession that there have been periods of my life during which I have been quite obsessed with food—of the class of pathetic character willing to drive thirty miles across the French countryside for a marginally more interesting plate of rabbit or whatever than I could get where I was. Wolf is likewise a well-mannered obsessive about food, whose dining table in Hamburg is admired and whose own approach to cooking is a fortunate combination of the robust elementalism of the food of his region and the elegance reflected in his pictures. One of the triumphs of my life was to have been asked by the *Good Food Guide* in London to become a "secret" inspector of restaurants for its annual report; unfortunately, I had to leave England shortly after this covert honor was bestowed and so could hardly indulge in the petty secret tyranny that is restaurant criticism and which I found so appealing.

Wolf and I have worked together before, first on an article for *Geo* magazine on the remarkable aesthetic and ritual features of the diet of the Japanese and the effect of their diet on their health. We found that we worked well and happily together, from our first meeting in the outstanding Okura Hotel in Tokyo. The article was awarded Gold Medals by the Art Directors Clubs of both America and Germany. Our next collaboration, again for *Geo*, was on the olive oil of Liguria, Italy, as well as on the people and region. I suppose it is unnecessary to record very extensively how fortunate I think I am to be able to work with such a gifted, amusing, and energetic artist, on subject matter that is as intriguing to think about as to savor. Adult work does not come much better.

It will come as no surprise to devotees of Chinese food and culture that there are those whose scholarship and skill are equal to the richness of the subject. Given our task here, it was not possible to discuss all that is involved in ideal detail and with the scholarly techniques, skill, and affection that fortunately are reflected in a variety of other useful publications. Those who want to pursue the subject in greater depth than this format allows can turn in full confidence to a few volumes that we have found particularly valuable. First, and the most useful of all, is *Food in Chinese Culture: Anthropological and Historical Perspectives*, K.C. Chang, editor: Yale University Press, 1977; and the recent study by Elizabeth Kroll: *The Family Rice Bowl*, published by United Nations Research Institute for Social Development, 1983. An especially friendly and informative cookbook that is more than a cookbook is by Barbara Tropp: *Modern Art of Chinese Cooking*, William Morrow, 1982. See also Kenneth Lo's *Regional Chinese Cookbook*, Larousse, New York, 1981.

Beijing (Peking)

Lanzhou

Suzhou

Wuxi

Chengdu

Wuhan

Shanghai

Lhasa

Hangzhou

Guilin

Kunming

Guangzhou (Canton)

Hong Kong

Contents

Introduction: China's Food   12

Such Imperial Food   24

River of Rice, River of Grain   40
    Recipes   63

Find the *Dofu* in this Picture   76
    Recipes   91

All China's Creatures   98
    Recipes   109

And All China's Wet Creatures   122
    Recipes   139

Medicine Food   150

To Market, to Market   166
    Recipes   205

Heat   214
    Recipes   227

中國食物

China's Food

中國食物

The world's biggest breakfast. The world's biggest lunch. The world's biggest dinner. All produced with that color, élan, variety, snap, crackle, and savor that have made the food of China so attractive and almost as common as the corner grocery store wherever the Chinese people have been allowed to live. Chinese cuisine achieved this stature not with the marketing muscle of McDonald's or Cadbury or General Foods or Nestlé, nor by any general strategy of gastronomic infiltration. Not even through the tangible if benign style of cultural imperialism with which French cuisine is associated. Rather, Chinese cuisine has prevailed essentially because of private decisions made by private people to open a storefront and sell cooked food in it. Which sells, and sells, and sells. People like it. More than like it. Many seem almost obsessed with it; they go on with hot loyalty about the new Chinese restaurant they have found just as they might talk about their lovers or richly amusing children.

A quarter of the world, over a billion people, eat nothing but Chinese food. That's their food. Millions more consume enough to sustain an often surprisingly intense fascination with it. Everyone wants the best, the most authentic, the most unexpected, the most various. Where is it? How can I get it? Does my town, my Chinatown, *really* have it? Am I being betrayed by compromising cooks who offer me what they think gringos will tolerate rather than what Chinese people adore? Do I get a pale imitation—Dvořák played on an adolescent's scratchy portable phono? Is it the dingy equivalent of that sloppy fallen angel, the dread continental cuisine? Or are there so many Chinese restaurants around the world because there is so much *good* Chinese food served in them?

Why not go to the source, to the mother of it, to see where it begins? That is, to the land of mystery and silk, of centuries of provocative isolation, of brilliant evocation of the past and magisterial claims in the political present. A country exploring the nature of socialism and the lure of private money. At once fiercely empirical in its attitude toward social life and wistfully poetic in its self-description. At once poor and promising, proud of its drama, ambivalent about its past, firm about its future. Country of a tumble of images: the crowded warrens and promenades of Shanghai, the sharp hill winds of Tibet, the thousand-year-old pagodas, last year's political poster. Terraced ranks of bushes of tea, rice stalks gathering size underwater, the Imperial this and the People's that, and again and always drama, distance, mystery.

And now, a place to go and be—where more and more cities are "open," which suggests that there is no military business to conceal and that, instead, there are at last suitable accommodations for visitors of other traditions—that it is no longer necessary for visitors to bend their ways and stoop their backs in order to move among the Chinese. It even becomes possible to travel as a cut-cost-to-the-bone individual traveler, so the posh hotels in out-of-the-way towns have begun sprouting backpacking students and grab-bag pilgrims, who come uneasily to the bar—they're not staying *at* the hotel, of course—to steal some time in the kind of environment they have left behind. And there are more (though not many) of the specialists in symbolic private quest, who, with firm, inner-lit eyes and brave beginner's Chinese, wait for days for the next available seat on a plane to Lhasa, the center of Tibet's mountain divinity.

Their private journey is understandable; truly there is a quality of fairy tale about the country, particularly the major old structures that survived the Cultural Revolution, which manage to haunt and revivify at once. The Summer Palace in Beijing (Peking) is as mysteriously uplifting as champagne, and as palatable and tangible. It wears its five hundred years with no apparent effort. It is not its size that commands, as in Westminster Abbey or St. Peter's, nor a fierce simplicity like that of Stonehenge, but rather its amazingly piled-on detail—its elaborate moldings, drawings, carvings, and complicated coloration—finally of giant intricacy. The palace and its grounds, its lake, its brilliant pier, and its pavilions gracefully accommodate far more people than were ever expected to be permitted into those gardens by the reclusive noble families that had them built—laboriously built, for a pittance, by the ancestors of those who, like me, now spend a Saturday afternoon wandering where all beheld is lovely.

The link between the people and the palace is important—it is also a vital connection in the food chain, part of the story that is expressed at table in the rice shop and the banquet room. The great cuisine of Chinese legend is royal and lavish, a tale of celebration told in paragraphs of foods of different colors, tastes, textures, temperatures, values, and *meanings*. But that cuisine hardly anyone in China eats often, though it is the defining myth by which all that's eaten is assessed. People eat the basic grains; what many foreigners treat as the essence of Chinese cuisine is for people there a desirable flavoring, a treat, almost a *rumor* of the "right stuff." It makes the rice or noodle tasty. It lends symbolic correctness to the matter of becoming sated.

In two major hotels in Beijing, the Beijing that is still the center of foreigners' life there, and the Fragrant Hills, designed by I. M. Pei and nestled gracefully in the parkland near the Summer Palace, the restaurant menus read in *almost* the usual way when translated: "Appetizers Hot, Appetizers Cold, Seafood, Fish, Poultry, Pork, Beef, Vegetables, Soups . . ." and "Food"! The latter refers to noodles, rice, buns, breads—the rice- and grain-based center of the Chinese meal. So central that at a banquet, wedding feast, or other celebration, rice or noodles are not served until the end of the cavalcade, to emphasize the luxury of the event and how different the cuisine is from the (literally) run-of-the-mill fare of daily life. The actual language reflects the reality, too—the word for "rice," *fan,* also means "food" and "meal;" it is as if the word for "food" were *Kartoffeln* in Germany, or *bread* in England.

It is hardly unusual for a society to be known by the culture of its kings and duchesses—hovels are atmospheric, but castles stimulate tourism. The same applies to food. Thus the worldwide elaborate appeal of the banquets available at the relatively few elegant restaurants left that recall directly the aristocratic system the Chinese have with some ferocity tried to excise. Of course, this has also resulted from the ample Chinese immigration to other countries; the Chinese restaurant business is labor-intensive, and there appears to be a ready supply of relatively inexpensive labor with which to conduct it—an economic reality, if an awkward one. (Consider the relationship between immigration patterns and the comparatively high cost of Japanese food prepared in North America and Europe.) But there seems little question that the international diner's interest in the food of China is based not only or even mainly on cost, but rather on the intrinsic taste and variety of what is served.

The traveler in China faces an additional variation on the problem of economic difference between diner and preparer. The China International Travel Service—the very thorough agency that governs all foreign travelers—tries to ensure that tourists generally come into contact with the most comfortable and sanitary facilities. For the visitor, inevitably this means entry into a world of great privilege, in comparison with the lives of the mass of Chinese people. In a sense, the tourist experiences the opposite of a revolution. Suddenly and willy-nilly, he or she is cast in the role of aristocrat, placed there by a community that has embraced the idea of equality as avidly as it is committed to rice and fireworks. He or she samples the finest of traditional Chinese cuisine, while students and workers gulp down bowls of rice moistened with a taste of pork in a salty sauce. So even the most modest and friendly visitor is at once privileged and exploited: privileged by being in a community where most people may earn four hundred dollars per year—perhaps the cost of a tourist's hotel room for a week—and exploited in that foreigners are charged twice as much as Chinese for domestic airplane tickets and far more for food when they order ahead and dine banquet-style. Granted, there is a considerable difference in the quality, quantity, and rarity of what is served; my impression was also that when Chinese people decide to eat high off the hog, they pay in their terms about the same amount as foreigners. And as to the vexing matter of the double-cost plane ticket, it must be said that ultimately this seemed reasonable and fair in practice if objectionable in theory—it is more than compensated for by the firm Chinese refusal to accept tips. It is difficult to realize how coercive—indeed, corrosive—the practice of tipping is until it becomes unnecessary and unthinkable. The endless nagging problems of how much, is it enough, why pay extra when it is undeserved, am I being too extravagant and thus foolish, are eliminated. What a relief.

Chinese Food, Essentially

The high cuisine the visitor to China enjoys during a formal dinner or a carefully ordered lunch is, of course, not the only form of it, and certainly not the most significant in daily life. As in any society, there is a different time and place for different styles and luxuriousnesses of food—the high and the low, the costly and the common, the once-a-year candy confection and the daily bread and bun, rice, and noodle. There is also a very highly developed set of ideas, theories, and near-religious beliefs about the use and meaning of food, the understanding of which has been the life's work of some very talented scholars and gourmets. How can we approach the almost endless variety of foods, styles, shapes, tastes, colors, that unite to form the cuisine of China?

One obvious way is perhaps the most common way, and that is to divide what one eats and sees by region, into the great broad styles of Chinese food: North (Beijing), South (Canton), East (Shanghai) and West (Hunan and Sichuan). Certainly that is the scheme used by many of the finest cookbooks, and the general guidebooks to the country evidently find this method useful, too. But for the visitor with limited time, and even for the more leisurely traveler, the division into strict zones of a variegated but nonetheless integrated nation becomes too arbitrary to do justice to the continuity between regions, the similarities among them, and the sense of family that the whole food culture shares. After all,

food is a kind of language, and if there is a successful and warmly embraced common language in China it is food. In spoken language, the differences in dialect are so great that someone from Shanghai may not understand a person from Sichuan, who may in turn find it awkward to converse with a compatriot from Harbin. But while there are regional preferences in food, and very different raw materials that are locally important in different ways, nevertheless there is a kind of food lexicon—a set of gastronomic building blocks or elements that keep recurring, perhaps in different ways, in different preparations, with this spice or that herb, here fried or there roasted. We propose to explore them here. There is also a lovely and strongly defined characteristic landscape within which the food is grown and transported, and we will try to make that come alive for you too.

The Context of Cuisine

A number of general observations come first. There is always a danger, when exploring a subject as vast and general as Chinese food and at the same time so intimately pleasing, of becoming a mere partygoer, a guest without any interesting criticism of one's hosts. We hope to maintain a degree of objectivity here. To celebrate a community so large is almost to celebrate human life in general. This is not a bad thing in itself, but it must in this case be joined to an appreciation of the endless daily intricacies involved in feeding this massive population, of trying to ensure that, each day, all the people of China have food to put into their mouths.

Another observation, if an obvious one, is that the Chinese way of eating is very much in keeping with the Chinese way of living. This bears remembering, because the communal sharing of food at table both compels and reflects a commitment to the social group that is graphically different from, for example, the arbitrary single plates of crafted food served to individuals in a Paris salon. That is, commitment is to the equity within the group, rather than to the aggressive indulgence of private preferences. As a result, the admired guest at a Chinese banquet should not allow anyone to know which are his or her most and least favorite dishes—to show strong partiality is simply inappropriate. Not that people do not eat lustily—quite the contrary. But the power of the group, to which personal appetite must appear to be subservient, persists, and so the ideal citizen eats sparingly of what he or she most enjoys.

No doubt this is to some extent a result simply of the phenomenal density of China. You will virtually never see nobody. People are always streaming by, on foot, on cycles, in buses, everywhere, always. In a desirable restaurant, etiquette dictates that a table be filled even with people who don't know one other—unlike in Europe and North America, where one diner often sits alone and the other place settings are removed lest anything violate the sacred privacy of Western man. And when a Chinese restaurant is crowded, there is no patient queue at the door, but a messier though effective arrangement: newcomers survey the house, estimate which diners are nearly done, and install themselves behind their chairs. China is also a country whose word for "good times" can also be used for "noisy," so there appears to be little concern with the acoustics of restaurants. It appears almost as if the intent is to keep the sound level high rather than muted and soft. Very little romantic cooing here! And the lights! Lights to do brain surgery under. Lights that distort the natural color of food and people. A cool, almost icy fluorescent style of lighting that manages somehow to be too bright and gloomy at the same time.

A word in general about decor and elegance, or the lack thereof. It is always worth remembering that there was a revolution in China in 1949, which, significantly, is called the Liberation by the Chinese. When I mistakenly used the word *revolution* to refer to it, it was assumed I meant the Cultural Revolution, the now much-despised enterprise of Mao Zedong and the Gang of Four, which included his wife and which was the occasion of rancorous arbitrary persecution of anyone thought to represent or to have profited from the bourgeois culture of the past. One countryman described to me his own sudden and forcible removal to a commune far from his home, where for four years he managed the pigpens, an exile he suffered, he said, because his father had owned a shop in a large city. Though he had never taken part in the business, the Party members who sent him away asserted that because of the business his family had been able to send him to a university. Thus he required penance to share fully the shiver of revolutionary zeal.

The remarkable excessiveness of the Cultural Revolution notwithstanding, the general process of breaking down the profound hierarchy of old China, with its centuries of rigid feudalism, still reflects itself not only in social activities but also in restrictions on the luxuries of the senses. The economic and social austerity of Mao's period was accompanied by a disdain for the elegant comforts of highfalutin' culture, and by a firm antipathy to any form of potentially demeaning service—the ricksha, for example, in which one person rode and was pulled by another. This also shows itself in the lack of attention to design and elegance of operation, even at restaurants claiming to serve desirable food and for which they charge relatively

large sums of money. For example, it is impossible to describe the crassness, meanness, abruptness, and dreadful food we had to endure at the most famous and largest Beijing duck restaurant in Beijing itself. (In contrast, the Beijing duck we were served at the Park Hotel in Shanghai was elegantly crisp, tasty, satisfying, charmingly served—wholly worthy of its reputation.) Certainly there are variations everywhere in how well and carefully restaurants or anything are managed; but the problem is exacerbated in China, because all enterprises are state-owned and until very recently there has been little incentive—at least in the form of higher earnings—to attend to the comfort of the clientele with any particular diligence or imagination. As a consequence, desultory time-serving mediocrity describes the work of many people, even in the famous food profession of China. At the same time, doubtless even politically severe Party officials still enjoyed their excellent food and exempted their own chefs from the general rules of lackluster life. A banquet we were given by the manager of the Shanghai guesthouse where Chairman Mao stayed—"After two days his room looked like a bookstore," he told us—suggested that Party leadership was no gastronomic-hardship post.

But now, as everyone is finding out, there are massive changes taking place, with new and strong pressures to give local autonomy and profit to individual enterprises so that good work and good service can be reflected directly in more income. Possibly it is in the food industry that the impact of the policy changes at the highest levels of Chinese society can be seen most vividly and extensively, if only because the results can be encountered three times a day, every day. It was difficult for me to imagine what Chinese cities looked like before the streets were opened to small vendors in the so-called free markets, which now jam the center of every city. How visually and gastronomically boring it must have been, having to acquire food at the equivalent of the Motor Vehicle Bureau of a colorless government. No fun, no fun at all. Whereas now the streets of Chinese cities are rich with things to peer at, poke at, fondle, try, and buy. Virtually everyone agrees that the food at the free markets is fresher and more interesting, to say nothing of more various, than what had been available before and what is currently shelved in the official state-owned shops. It will be fascinating to observe the impact of such competition on an increasingly demanding public with disposable yuan in their pockets.

Perhaps because refrigeration and other forms of preservation have been relatively rare (except for pickling), the Chinese insist on the freshest of ingredients. These include chickens, fish, crabs, ducks—practically the whole farm. The markets are a riot of unfortunate, irritated, incarcerated creatures squawking and splashing, soon to become someone's dinner. The street will be the last home of a vigorously complaining pig tied to a cart, or a cackling chicken tied to a rickety bike, or a fish flopping around on soaked newsprint. And some markets are even more colorful, perhaps so much so as to disturb the visitor of merely average squeamishness. In the Guangzhou (Canton) food market, for example, you will see snakes, birds, dogs, weasels, rabbits, and even a basketful of playful kittens. Will the last be bought to catch mice? Or to be eaten themselves, if not now then later when they are fatter? I confess I didn't ask and didn't want to know.

The intensity of the street markets has got to be experienced to be appreciated. The smells, the sounds, the feel of the pavement, the pressure of bodies and food stands, the colors and the commotion—all become part of an exhausting, vital fray that it is difficult to imagine any government could successfully ban. And yet Mao's government did just that, because free-marketers were "capitalist-roaders" whose willfulness and prosperity would call into question the purity and meaning of the Chinese experiment. They would cause envy and inequality. They would stimulate a diverting of scarce resources, from the public sectors where the almighty planners thought they should go, to the private lives of Chinese people whose enjoyments and joys were to be secondary to the vaunted scheme of the greater empire of the future. Austerity would purify, prudence would educate, the parsimony of the people in private would yield the public luxuries of roads, steel mills, effective defense forces, the apparatus of contemporary government—in essence, the strong platform on which would be built a modern economy that could support a powerful and respected China, able to assume the place in the sun that its history and population allowed it to claim.

This lasted for a while, under the usual watchfulness of a totalitarian regime. But recently there has been a major shift, the immense significance of which, both for China and for the very idea of how communism and modern industry can interact in a developing country, is now beginning to be clear. For example, during the period I was in China, in the autumn of 1984, a Congress of remarkable consequence announced that the leaders of the Party had been wrong in the past, that they had confused ownership of the means of production with their management, and that the new look in Chinese economy required unleashing those very private enterprising forces that had formerly been the sign of accursed and unoriginal sin. And this was announced in the government's own press. The impact was palpable.

What impressed me about the Party leaders' *nostra culpa* was the robust pragmatism of the development and its rather understated emotional charge. Business-as-unusual was the new order of the day. It began to seem as if the value of the pursuit of wealth was self-evident. As if it would, almost all by itself, lead to the better, more just society for which the Grand Old Men and Women of the Liberation had so patiently and presciently struggled. As if efficient and productive work was in itself a kind of redemption, almost a sign of grace. As if individuals working on their and their families' behalf would nonetheless end up accomplishing what was best for everyone. But the impact of all this may very well be different. For example, despite the Government's very firm position on family planning—one child per couple is the legal norm—the economic value of more children is likely to be so great for farmers that they will be willing to overlook the fines and other penalties for having them. And school boards are currently confronting increasing delinquency among schoolchildren. Not because they are playing hooky—they are minding their parents' ducks and geese!

The Politics of the Mouth

It seems that Adam Smith's "unseen hand" is operating a wok. The politics of the mouth can be seen very clearly in the street markets. It is echoed in the new prosperity of the peasants who have alacritously moved to supply these markets, often so well and providently that they are becoming rich—the government press (which is, broadly speaking, the only one) proudly announces the evidently exemplary triumphs of families whose income from eggs or transport or produce or whatever has yielded them as much as ten thousand yuan a year, or twenty-five times the average income of the average peasant. A few incomes of this sort in a country of a billion people may make relatively little practical difference at first. But the symbolic impact is already enormous, the more so because the government-controlled press is fully deployed to make widely known the good fortune of these new plutocrats.

Someone said an army runs on its stomach, and so, apparently, can a new political order. Coffee-in-the-bean has made its appearance in a few groceries in Shanghai, to the evident surprise of visitors who had not seen this foreign luxury there before. (This doesn't mean that the coffee lover who visits China will no longer need to bring a jar of tolerable instant with which to spike the brew-by-the-name-coffee offered in the morning.) Not that what is Western is necessarily desirable: I was annoyed to discover that my hotels assumed I'd prefer a "Western breakfast" to the much more interesting and informative Chinese one. Nevertheless, the coffee issue may reveal an opening up of China to the world in food terms as well as industrially.

So far this has not taken the most obvious and clamorous forms, such as the introduction of Western-style fast-food chains. (When McDonald's opened its first shop in Tokyo—the Tokyo of brilliant classical cuisine—it served so many hamburgers that its cash register burned itself out; the chain opens a shop somewhere in the world every sixteen hours.) Given China's radical recent history, though, it is bizarre that the first major "franchise" outlet should be Maxim's of Paris, which opened to serve meals costing the average Chinese person the equivalent of three to four month's wages—echoing the decadent elegant Paris so antithetical to the spirit of Mao, his Long March, and the realities of Chinese economic life.

Of course Chinese food is the original "fast food;" the constraints of scarce fuel necessitate the chopped-up constituents of the cuisine. Generally it cooks quickly and retains its nutritional qualities; and chopping and dicing expose the maximum surface area to cooking and flavoring agents, yielding the most flavor from the least raw material.

All of this (plus the afore-mentioned traditional shortage of refrigeration) places a premium on fresh ingredients of good quality. Also, there is relatively little raw food served in China (unlike Japanese cuisine, for example)—not as salad or sushi or anything comparable. Since an important element of Chinese agriculture is the use of "night soil," human excrement used as fertilizer, there is real danger of infectious transmission unless food is thoroughly and appropriately cooked. So food is cooked very hot, just as drinking water is generally boiled. But the cooking techniques used must combine this concern about health with a commitment to tasty freshness and the conservation of fuel. Better a person should spend that heretofore ample resource, time, chopping and slicing than that hard cash be expended for wood, charcoal, or another fuel.

Or at least until recently—until the surge of prosperity and activity following the remarkable changes in Chinese economic life that the Deng Xiaoping government began to introduce in 1978. People are earning more money, and so, ironically, they want to work more and therefore have less time for the shopping and cooking that they formerly had no economic choice but to do. As a result, the Chinese government is beginning to anticipate the emergence of a powerful convenience-food industry, and in 1984 it invested as much money in the food industry as it had in the previous thirty years combined. Output of fast-food packages has quadrupled since 1980 in major cities, and the nation's third fast-food restaurant opened in 1984 in Beijing and serves some eight thousand people daily. This is not altogether gargantuan, though, when we consider that what is thought to be the finest restaurant in Guangzhou seats two thousand, has four stories, and burgeons with people throughout the day. And, as I can affirm, the quality is high. So there is not necessarily going to be a war between quality and quantity.

Nevertheless, the inevitable complaints have already been registered about the relatively high cost and lack of flavor of industrially prepared food, and there is little question that the greater time pressures will begin to affect how the Chinese eat, and in turn what they eat.

But that is the uncertain future. Let us turn to the vivid present. We confront a vast and varied country whose food is one of the most attractive and well-traveled of the world's cuisines. It has a necessarily intimate connection with Chinese history and its turbulent, dramatic, often violent political structure. Yet the food stands on its own too, as tasty artifact, source of pleasure, an elegant language to read and try to speak oneself. And some of this can be absorbed with our human eyes. 福

这样的皇宫食物

Such

Imperial

Food

Many elements conspire to give a culture of profound complexity its special mark, its characteristic assertion about the nature of human life, what should be emphasized, what denied, what embraced, what kept at arm's length. In China the Forbidden City in Beijing reveals in lacquered wood, metal, stone, and, perhaps most subtly of all, in paint and gilt how its creators and owners perceived the symbolic world; in what rhythms they thought the eye best able to confront the truth of material objects; how they felt about the emperor; what they dreamed was real. And those images are inescapably still part of the whole world's idea of China—and basic to contemporary Chinese life, even the political part of it that derives its energy from pressing hard for clear change from the unfair old days.

The images are asserted in the subtlest of ways, as I realized in the very first moments of my time in China. After a trip of nearly twenty-four hours, I landed at midnight in Beijing and took a taxi to my hotel. The cab radio was offering a rendition of Beethoven's Ninth Symphony by the Shanghai Orchestra. There was a mysterious quality to the music, as if it had been passed on from musician to musician between Bonn and Beijing and had emerged with a definably Chinese sound, even while all the notes being played were the same familiar ones, on the same familiar instruments. There I was, in the soft, humid autumn night, noticing large golden leaves splattered across the roadway and the trees and shapes that loomed in silence alongside, and in an instant a signature feature of my native culture had been subtly and firmly pressed into a new form.

So with the food. Perhaps it is true that for the Chinese today the reality of daily eating is remote from the brilliance of traditional arrangements and the phenomenal variety of creations of Imperial cuisine. Nevertheless, it remains an encapsulating presence, because there is a theory in Chinese cuisine that derives from that classical tradition so intertwined with Imperial power.

Many non-Chinese know of yin and yang, the components of the classical notion of balance—the idea that the universe is not random but forms itself into discernible principles. Yin involves innerness, a sense of yielding and accommodating to the world, elements of femininity. Yang is assertive, rougher, harder, shows elements of masculinity. There is a complementarity here, and the two must fulfill each other respectfully; otherwise, there will be disorder and foolishness in countless aspects of life. This is a daily matter in China. Good and appropriate foods, for example, reflect the variety the Chinese require for the healthful, measured life. Not just hot and cold or sweet and sour, but also forceful and tender, crunchy and smooth, light and heavy. One reason for there being so many dishes at one time on the Chinese table is so that the diner can appreciate the variety and contrast the cook has orchestrated into the meal.

Also, the firm impact of mythology makes it de rigueur that a decent banquet boast a dragon and phoenix, created out of foods crafted to look like what they are not. There is, indeed, a whole sense of odd play and sometimes whimsical transformation in the Chinese kitchen—to make things such as duck feet look like fish fins, for example—that is in sharp contrast to the general rule that foods must be fresh and cooked to reveal their essence and their most persuasive character. This is luxurious sport, and it took the wealth of Imperial China to go in for it with avidity. However, a community's choice of luxuries may also tell us what its necessities are. There seems little doubt that the Chinese people regard their food as storied, not just literal. This attitude may well have been one animating reason for the creativity in the cuisine itself, for the intensity of its coloration, its often wild mixtures, its vigorous variation. And even if philosophy is not the main concern of the diner relishing a traditional banquet, he or she is never far from an elaborate view of the world tied tightly to the arrangement of life known as Imperial China. 福

A fifteenth-century masterpiece. Made without nails, the huge dome of fifty thousand glazed tiles is supported by twenty-eight columns hewn from trees collected in Yunnan. This Hall of Prayer for Good Harvests was visited by the emperor and his entourage each year before the winter solstice. Both architecture and decoration are densely symbolic.

29

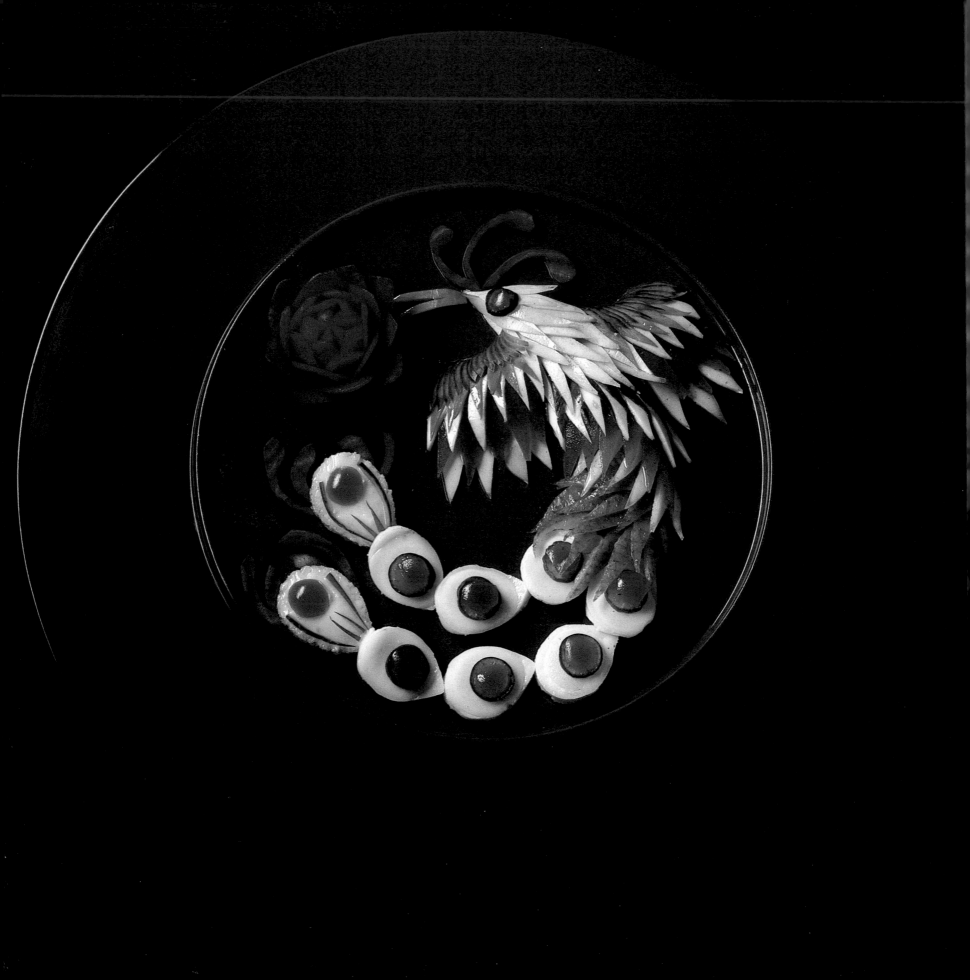

In the same restaurant, a dragon created with carrot, egg yolk, beef, and cucumber graces a banquet table.

These two dishes are typical of the Imperial tradition, which combines the edible and the symbolic. In fact, all one has to do is turn back to the photo of the Great Temple (page 29), and there on the pillars are the same two animal representations—in a very different context.

Dishes made to look like images in a sacred temple. Food that was always more than food. This was Imperial China.

A phoenix from the Fangshan restaurant of Beijing. It is made of duck's skin, pigeon eggs, beet, egg whites, and cucumber.

Sweets from Beijing's Fang-shan restaurant: puff pastry with sweet bean paste above sticky rice sculpted into "Buddha's Hands."

From the Nanlin restaurant in Suzhou, a sticky rice decoration shaped like a peacock.

This "lantern" was prepared in Wuxi. It's made of shrimp, egg, tangerine, and fried spinach in a tomato-based sauce.

A duck's webbed foot becomes the tail fin of a stylized fish molded of ground chicken meat! A provocative artifice.

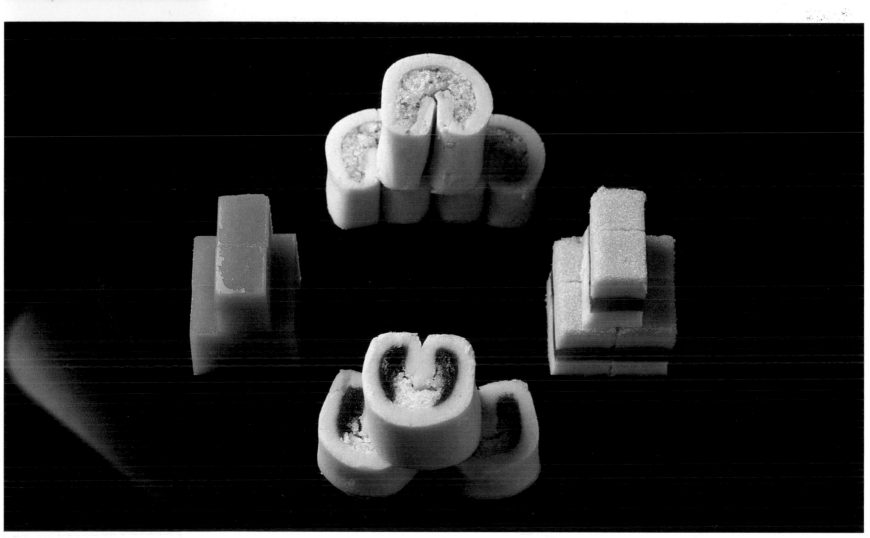

Imperial sweets from Beijing. Made of green peas, wheat flour, and filled with red bean paste.

Another example of Chinese enthusiasm for the playful transformation of food into symbolic creatures: a sticky rice fish from the Nanlin restaurant in Suzhou.

More decorative transformations.

A crane carved from a pumpkin highlights a festive meal at the Hubin in Wuxi. The hotel is on Lake Taihu, where fishermen abound.

A dessert made from fresh berries and milk mixed with ground almonds, formed into the "yin-yang" symbol of balance in all things.

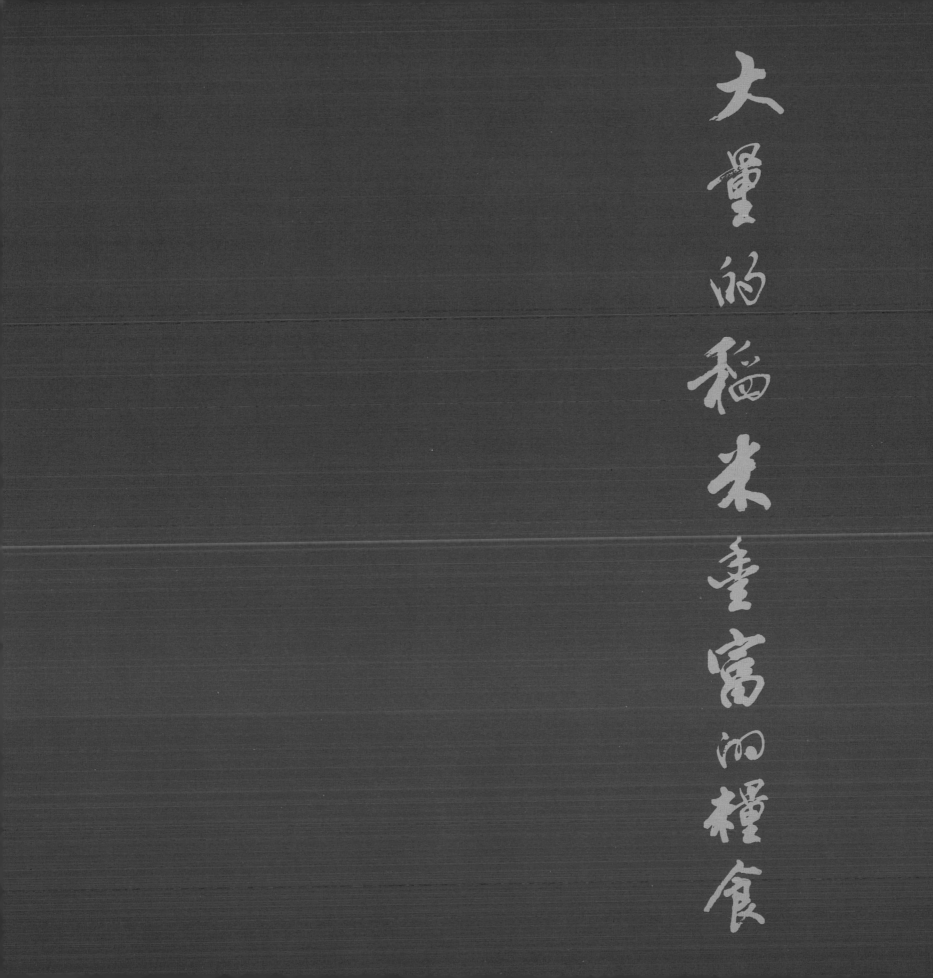

大量的稻米產量富饒的糧食

River
of
Rice,
River
of
Grain

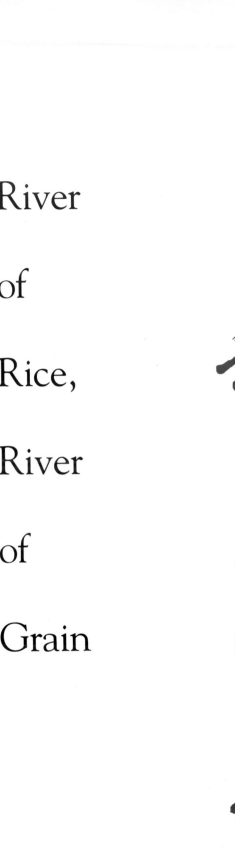

A quarter of the planet's people live in China, but they must feed themselves on only seven percent of the world's arable land. The result: hardly any of the land is left alone. Every possible inch boasts a plant. So cultivated is the country, it is almost appropriate to say that there are no landscapes, only farmscapes. Farmscapes of quite breathtaking complexity and size— earth sculptures a thousand years old, every square inch providing a few mouthfuls of sustenance. In northern China, intricately boundaried fields of wheat often provide the basic stuff. In the southern half, rice grows along the famous mountain terraces and flat in brooding ponds. Growing rice yields more nutritional value (per acre) than any equivalent crop; it is said that in southern China more people are fed by an acre than anywhere else in the world, and the region is widely regarded as among the most successful worldwide at commercial cultivation of a wide variety of crops.

The thousand-year-old task endures, to feed the millions, the tens of millions, the hundreds of millions, three times a day. The ancient systems of irrigation and the intricate terraces along which water flows in scrupulously gentle inclines are monuments to centuries of experimentation and knowledge about how best to live on and with this land. No one could have done this alone, as a homesteader or an isolated enterprise. A large group is the smallest unit that could have solved the problems irrigation presented, and perhaps this is the basis of traditional Chinese communalism.

Rice (*fan*) and grain are at the heart of the matter; China is the world's largest producer of food grains. Many writers find the concept of "elegant variation"–changing the form, the words, the pacing of sentences–useful. The same idea applies to the way Chinese cooks approach their task of feeding people, often with very limited ingredients and often with the same ones over and over again. Sometimes the result is a mysterious and dazzling process in which the grain (in particular) seems to disappear, only to return as something else altogether. It gets boiled, steamed, fried, baked, pushed, pulled, twisted, filled, wrapped, flattened, tied, dried. It is found in everything from the breakfast doughnut in a Beijing street stall to the elegant fluted pastry of a diplomatic banquet, so in the north the elegant variation is of the grain itself. In the south, where there is more rice, the focus of variation is more on what is *added* to the rice–the sharp pickles, the strongly spiced and sauced meats, fish, vegetables; even if the grains of rice are the same, the mouth is surprised.

And the *fan* is everywhere. It dries on straw mats at the sides of roads, it is carried in sacks on the backs of porters or perched precariously on the ubiquitous bicycles that, like strange long insects, populate China. During the Sui dynasty, from 581 to 618 A.D., the Imperial Canal was built to connect three rivers–the Haihe, the Huang He or Yellow, and the Chang Jiang or Yangtze–among other reasons, to make it easier to transport rice from the fertile south to the north, which is comparatively drier and had developed hardier strains of wheat more difficult to farm. To this day stately trains of ten or more grain barges can be seen gliding along the water. On days when the farmers deliver rice to the government warehouses for distribution throughout China, long lines of people on foot or in a variety of vehicles, like peasants of old and like peasants forever, wait resignedly for their turn with the officials. In the late 1970s rice was rationed, and people abided by the limit: office workers received less than manual laborers, heavy laborers more than anyone, children according to their age. But now there is enough rice, in some areas more than enough, and so the ration coupons mean less or nothing, and shoppers can easily obtain what they need in the free markets.

An Associated Press dispatch from Beijing on December 27, 1984: "China's granaries are overflowing after a record harvest . . . more than state grain stores can accommodate." More than enough rice in China! A monumental fact in the modern world! 福

Harvesting rice among
unique rocky columns near
Guilin, a tiny fragment of
an endless fairy-tale landscape, hundreds of miles
wide. A legacy of geological
thrust and 300 million
years of erosion.

Wheat grows on man-made
terraces of two-thousand-
meter-high mountains near
Lanzhou, in Gansu
province.

Buddha in a rice field near
Shaoxing.

Harvesting near Guilin.

A view from an almost un-
reachable village of the six
hundred-year-old rice
terraces of the Zhuang people, the largest ethnic minor-
ity in China. Near Guilin.

Harvesting barley near
Lhasa, in Tibet.

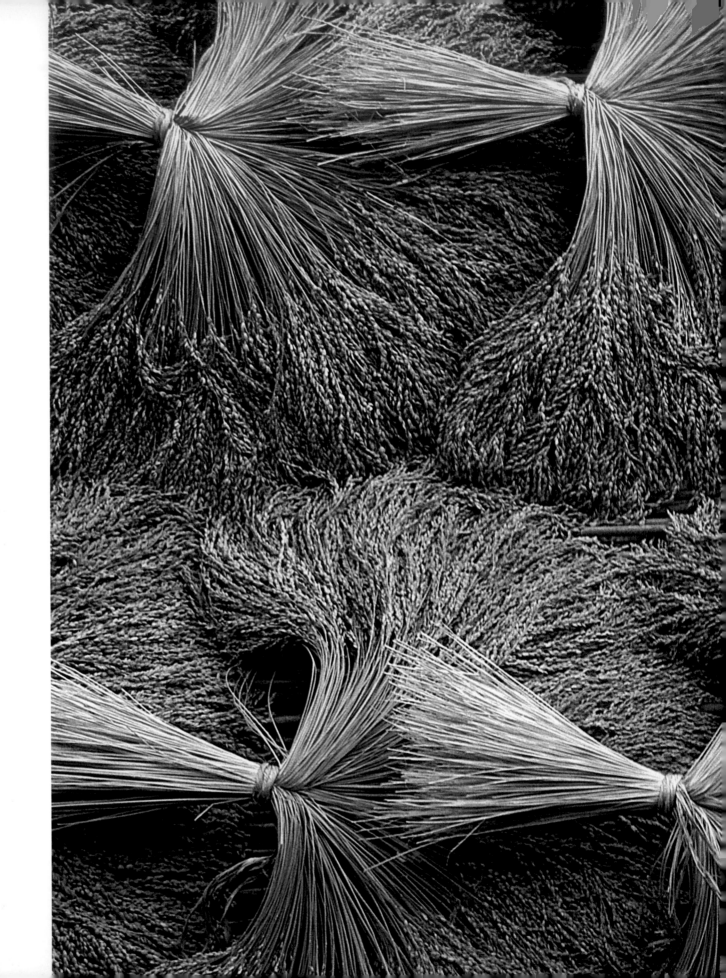

The Zhuang people bundle their rice in the field, dry these bundles in the sun, and store them unthreshed for the winter.

Harvesting rice near
Guilin.

A young man carries rice
to his wooden home. He
dries the rice in the sun on
the roof of his house and
stores it in bundles like this.

Wheat noodles hanging on bamboo poles outside a noodle factory in Guilin.

An "elegant variation"—
wheat flour fan-shaped and
deep-fried in a Chengdu
market. Either a snack or
as breakfast, with hot soybean milk.

Chinese "ravioli" from
Yunnan province, filled with
a green-vegetable-and-pork
mixture.

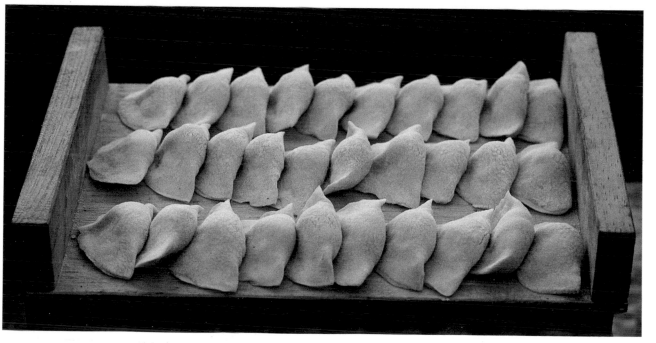

Jiaozi, or dumplings. One of
the most popular foods in
China. From a small restaurant in Hangzhou.

A child's treat—sweet, deep-fried sticky rice balls—sold from the back of the omnipresent bicycle.

More variation. Twisted and deep-fried wheat-flour sticks commonly eaten for breakfast, often with hot soybean milk.

A wheat-flour variation, this time a deep-fried triangle filled with sweet bean paste.

The ubiquitous *baozi*. Served with a dash of soy sauce and hot-chili oil.

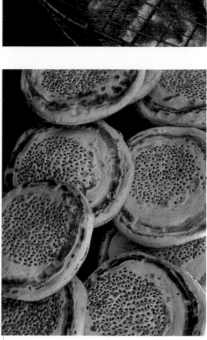

Flat wheat bread baked on a clay mold in the "free market" of a village near Chengdu, in Sichuan province.

Deep-fried cakes from Shanghai, made of sticky rice flour and filled with sweet red bean paste.

Rice

For many beginners perhaps the most mystifying of cooking preparations is that basic Chinese staple—properly cooked rice. Good rice is really very easy to prepare. Here is a virtually foolproof method for creating fine rice.

Use extra long-grain rice, preferably Texas-grown. Wash it 3 or 4 times. As you rinse it, rub it between your hands.

Drain well after washing. Then add water and let rice sit for 2 hours before cooking.

A good ratio is 1 cup of rice to 7½ ounces of water for 2 people. So-called "old rice," that which has been lying about in sacks for long periods, will absorb more water and will be easier to cook.

Begin cooking uncovered over high heat. Stir with chopsticks and cook for about 4 minutes. Water evaporates and rice will continue to be quite hard. Cover the pot and cook over low heat for about 8 minutes more, stirring from time to time.

Well-cooked rice will have absorbed the water but will not be lumpy, nor will the kernels stick together. They will be firm and fluffy.

After turning off the heat source, loosen rice with chopsticks. This will help retain fluffiness. Cover tightly until ready to serve. Just before serving, stir rice with chopsticks once again.

Pancakes

(Bok Bang)

1¾ cups flour (high gluten)
½ cup flour (for dusting)
¾ cup water, brought to a boil
1½ teaspoons sesame oil

■Place flour in mixing bowl and add boiling water. Mix with two pairs of chopsticks or a wooden spoon in the same direction continuously. When dough absorbs water and cools, place on a work surface dusted with flour. Knead until dough is thoroughly mixed, about 2 minutes. Place in a mixing bowl and cover with plastic wrap, allow to sit for ½ hour.

■Roll into a 12-inch sausage. Divide into 12 equal pieces. Dust surface again with flour and flatten each piece with the palm of your hand. Use more flour to dust if dough sticks. Use plastic wrap to cover unused dough.

■Working with 2 pieces at a time, wipe top of one gently with sesame oil and place the other flattened piece on top. Dust with flour if necessary and roll them into circles 7 inches in diameter. The result will be a 2-layer pankcake.

■Heat wok over low-medium heat for about 1 minute. Place pancake into hot, dry wok, cook 1 minute or until pancake begins to bubble up. Turn over. When pancake is cooked a few brown spots will be visible. Remove from wok and separate the two layers. You will have two pancakes, each browned lightly on one side. Repeat until finished.

■When ready to use, steam pancakes 5 to 7 minutes and serve.

Note: Heat in the dry wok must be carefully controlled. If too high, pancakes will burn and not cook properly. (Pancakes can be made well ahead of time. They can be frozen—allow to defrost before steaming.)

Yield: 12 pancakes

Pan-fried Noodles with Pork and Scallions

½ pound thin fresh egg
   noodles (vermicelli)
1 teaspoon salt
1¼ cups scallions (use white
   portions and tender parts
   of green)
6 ounces fresh, lean pork,
   shredded
1¼ teaspoons minced garlic
4½ tablespoons peanut oil

Make a marinade:
½ teaspoon ginger juice
   mixed with ½ teaspoon
   white wine
¼ teaspoon salt
½ teaspoon sugar
½ teaspoon light soy sauce
½ teaspoon sesame oil
1½ teaspoons oyster sauce
pinch of white pepper
1 teaspoon cornstarch

Make a sauce:
¾ teaspoon sugar
½ teaspoon dark soy sauce
2 teaspoons oyster sauce
1 teaspoon sesame oil
1 tablespoon cornstarch
1 cup chicken broth

■In separate bowls combine ingredients for marinade and sauce, and reserve.

■Cook noodles for 10 seconds in a large pot of boiling water (6 cups) with 1 teaspoon salt. Add cold water to noodles, then drain. Refill pot with cold water and drain again. Repeat twice more. Place noodles in a strainer to drain thoroughly for 1 to 1½ hours.

■Place shredded pork in marinade. Set aside for 30 minutes.

■Wash and dry scallions, slice thinly and cut into 1½-inch lengths. Set aside.

■In a large frying pan (preferably cast iron) heat 3 tablespoons of peanut oil over high heat. When a wisp of white smoke appears, add noodles to the pan. Spread evenly. Cook 1 minute over high heat, then lower heat and move pan about the burner to allow edges of noodles to cook evenly. Cook about 10 minutes or until noodles are light brown. If noodles stick to pan, add more oil. Turn noodles and repeat.

■Heat wok over high heat. Add 1½ tablespoons of peanut oil. Using a spatula, coat the wok with the oil, and add garlic. When garlic turns brown, add pork. Spread pork in a thin layer and cook 2 to 3 minutes. Turn the pork over, and repeat until it turns white. Add scallions and mix thoroughly. Stir the sauce, make a well in the center of the pork mixture, and pour into the well. Stir and mix. When the mixture thickens and turns brown, turn off heat.

■Spread noodles on serving dish, place the pork and scallions mixture on top and serve.

Yield: 6 servings

Steamed

Buns

The dough for these buns, with a bleached flour base, is ideal to create several varieties of Cantonese *dim sum* or simply steamed without fillings—perfect for making those buns favored as accompaniments to meals in Peking. Once the dough has been cooked through, it becomes soft and spongelike. It accommodates fillings of roast pork, lotus seed paste, red bean paste and Chinese sausage quite well.

3½ cups flour
5¼ teaspoons baking powder
¾ cup sugar
4½ ounces milk
2¼ ounces water
3 tablespoons lard

■Mix flour, baking powder and sugar together on a work surface, then make a well in the middle. Add milk gradually and, with your fingers, combine with the flour mixture. After milk has been absorbed, add water and continue to work the dough.

■Add lard and, again with your fingers, continue to work the dough.

■Using the dough scraper, gather the dough with one hand and begin kneading with the other hand. Knead for 12 to 15 minutes. If dough is dry, add 1 teaspoon of water at a time and continue to knead until the dough becomes elastic. If the dough is wet, sprinkle a bit of flour on the work surface and on your hands and continue working.

■When dough is elastic, cover with a moderately damp cloth and allow dough to rest for about 1 hour. Then divide in 2 equal parts.

■Roll dough pieces into 2 cylinders, each about 10 inches long. Cut each cylinder into 10 equal pieces. Form each piece into a rectangle about 2½ by 3½ inches and place on a piece of waxed paper 3½ by 4½ inches, so that there is a ½-inch border of waxed paper showing. Repeat until all 20 buns are formed.

■Place buns in a bamboo steamer and steam in a wok over boiling water for 15 to 20 minutes, until buns become spongy and aquire a glistening glaze. Remove from steamer and serve immediately.

Yield: 20 buns

Preserved vegetables from
the market in Kunming offer
different flavors to the rice
to which they are added.
Each region, and even
each family, has a characteristic way of preserving its
local vegetables.

Filling rice is another way of
adding different tastes to it.
Here, dried plums mixed
with pork and sticky rice,
wrapped in bamboo leaves
and steamed for about two
hours.

A dish made out of four different kinds of noodles:
handmade, broad, thin, and
egg.

One of the innumerable ways of transforming a pouch of transparent wheat flour into a distinct dish. Here, minced shrimp *dim sum* from Guangzhou (Canton), steamed for breakfast and presented on jade chopsticks.

Moon cakes. Exchanged at the time of the mid-autumn Buddhist Moon Festival in September and for family celebrations. Decorated with floral designs or inscriptions—"double happiness," says the moon cake in the middle—and filled with red bean paste, sweet sesame seeds, and lotus seeds. The others contain salty pork, egg yolk, and chicken.

在這照片中見豆腐

Find the Dofu in This Picture

Of course *dofu* (tofu) is bean curd, a foodstuff almost mysteriously uninteresting in its original state, so bland and so imposingly uniform that it seems the ideal product of a futuristic dictatorship committed to the denial of fun, the perfect food for a country managed by depressed chemical engineers who relish standardization. Indeed, it *is* produced in factories, even if they aren't *big* ones and don't belch smoke.

It is impossible to overestimate *dofu's* importance to the Chinese diet—it is the most inexpensive basic protein source and mercifully low in cholesterol—or the ingenuity of cooks who have found an array of intriguing ways to prepare it. From the simple bean emerges an edible of endless use and value that is perhaps the nutritional cornerstone of the Chinese diet. And the triumphant development of this food is a dramatic example of the close and provident connection between the land and the people.

Virtually everywhere in China there is a particular *mapu dofu*—a "home-style" *dofu*. Because it is so bland, it responds readily to the flavors and textures that surround it, so it reflects well whatever region it is prepared and eaten in. And this is everywhere, because it is such an inexpensive and ecologically sound source of vital protein. Meat, fish, and even flavorful vegetables have been luxuries for much of China for most of its history. The North American and European idea of the Chinese meal, that is, various plates full of substantial food, is a vast exaggeration, and the "side dishes" of rice or noodles or rolls are closer to the truth. But *dofu* is relatively easy to grow and produce. Because it is a living substance, it must be used fresh—*dofu* vendors deliver it to the home, like milk. Because of its malleable texture, it is often carved (with striking fidelity) into the mock meats and poultry that almost inevitably adorn the table for a Buddhist vegetarian feast. This is usually the obsessive task of monks with lifetimes on their hands, and the skill for the task, but this is another, if minor, reason for the ubiquity of the food and its elaborate role in the culture of Chinese food. And because it serves as such a neutral starting point, it poses a particular challenge to cooks at home and in restaurants.

It is surprisingly difficult to gain admission to the inside of a Chinese enterprise, particularly one that smacks of tradition, that is not "up-to-date," not representative of the "Four Modernizations" that the current government has embraced as its goals (the accelerated development of agriculture, industry, national defense, and science and technology called for in 1975). So it was through a stroke of luck, not by design, that we got to explore the inside of a *dofu* factory, in a small town near Chengdu (Chengtu), the capital of the Sichuan province. We saw it as the shafts of late-afternoon sun lighted its wood-buttressed inner structure, and gave us the secrets of *dofu*, the unalarming secrets. At last we had seen one of the places from which this substance emerged.

And what did the secrets of *dofu* turn out to be? At the back and top of the structure were sacks of beans, several varieties. These were emptied into huge vats of water for soaking, and once they were plump with water the beans were cooked in still other vats. At that point edible lime was added to the mixture, and fermentation began. When the appropriate amount of curdling had occurred, the mixture was run into wooden and textile containers (which leave a curiously faithful impression on it—take a look at your next neat curd), and the liquid, or "milk," was pressed out, to be used on its own. Then the curds were fashioned into cakes, as big as the honey cakes found at weddings, and whisked off for their famous quick delivery to wherever *dofu* was needed that day.

Happily do I remember those shafts of afternoon sunlight, the brisk activity, the many genuine smiles. What a strong sense there was of the elementalism of the making of it! Not surprising, given the almost ludicrous simplicity of the food itself. 福

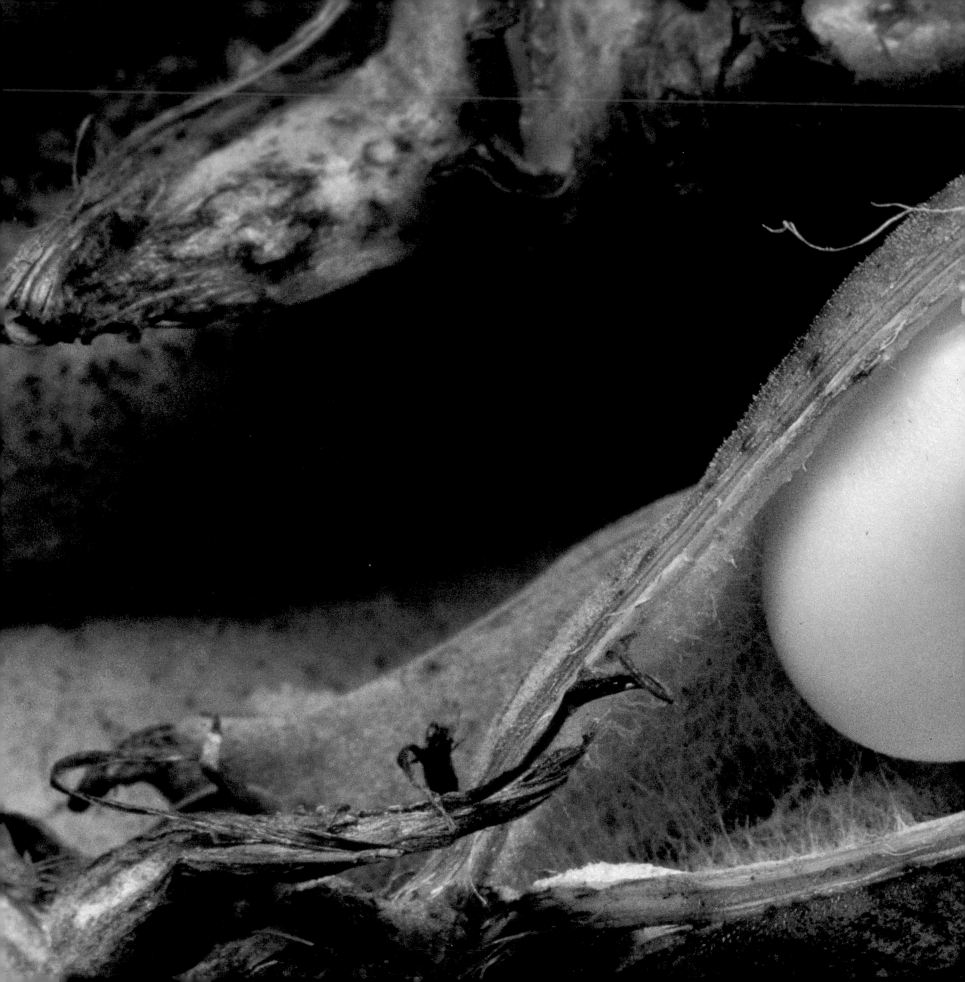

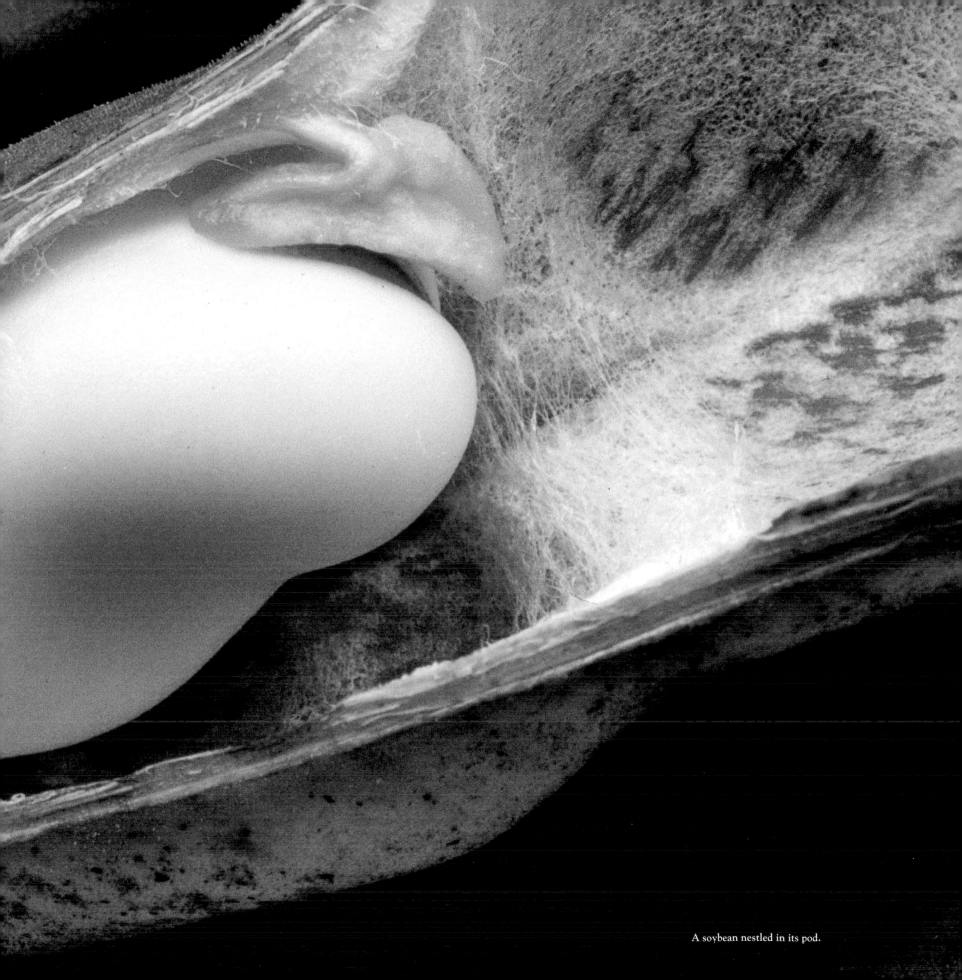

A soybean nestled in its pod.

Cakes of *dofu* in a Sichuan
market, kept fresh for the
customer with cubes of wood.

A view of a market basket in Sichuan, filled with thin sheets of half-dried *dofu* used for wrapping meat or added to soup, and *dofu* "sausages" made of half-dried bean curd.

Dofu in sheets.

Dofu in the form of noodles,
for soup.

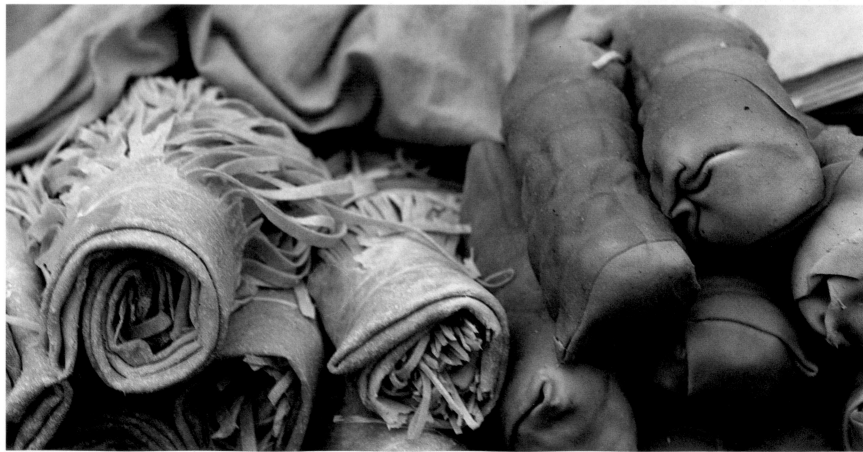

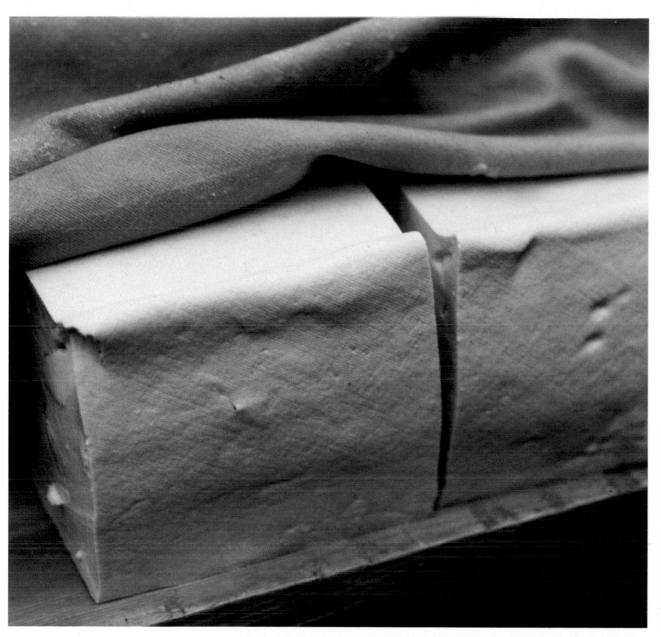

The most common form of *dofu*.

A *dofu* specialty of Yunnan province that is allowed to molder and is then fried before consumption.

Soft *dofu*, kept in water.

Chengdu specialties-
smoked *dofu* in different-
size squares for sale in the
free market.

A collage of Sichuan *dofu*.
Rolled and thin, smoked
and dried, smoked and big,
spicy and small...

Various kinds of *dofu*,
all bought in the
Lanzhou market.

Pan-fried
Dofu
with
Mushrooms

Dofu can be kept from 2 to 3 weeks in a plastic container, in water, provided the water is changed daily. It must be refrigerated.

6 small cakes of fresh *dofu* (thoroughly dried with paper towels)
½ pound fresh mushrooms (wiped clean with paper towels, stems removed, and each cap cut into 3 pieces)
2 to 3 tablespoons peanut oil (to fry *dofu*)
1½ tablespoons peanut oil mixed with ¼ teaspoon salt (to fry mushrooms)

Sauce:
1½ tablespoons cornstarch
2 tablespoons dark soy sauce
¼ to ½ teaspoon salt
1 teaspoon sugar
1 cup of vegetable stock or cold water

10 sprigs of coriander

■In a large pot bring 3 cups of water to a boil. Add mushrooms, bring water back to a boil. Remove pot from heat, run cold water in, then strain off all water. Drain mushrooms and set aside.

■Heat in a flat-bottomed frying pan (preferably cast iron) 2 to 3 tablespoons peanut oil. Fry *dofu* cakes for 5 to 7 minutes, or until light brown. Turn cakes over and repeat. Both sides should be light brown. Place in a serving dish and cut into 1-inch pieces.

■Heat wok over high heat, add 1½ tablespoons peanut oil mixed with salt. Stir-fry mushrooms for 30 seconds.

■Stir sauce ingredients and add to wok over low heat. Continue stirring clockwise until sauce thickens and becomes dark brown. Pour sauce and mushrooms over *dofu*, garnish with sprigs of coriander, and serve immediately.

Yield: 6 to 8 servings

Note: For those who prefer an alternative, the *dofu* can be steamed and served in the same way.

6 small cakes of fresh *dofu*
(well-drained, patted dry
with paper towels, cut into
½-inch dice)
4 ounces ground pork
4 dried chili peppers
½ teaspoon minced ginger
½ teaspoon minced garlic
1 tablespoon chili paste
3 tablespoons peanut oil
1 teaspoon sesame oil
1 scallion, washed, dried,
finely sliced

Sauce:
¼ teaspoon salt
1 teaspoon sugar
2 teaspoons light soy sauce
1 teaspoon dark soy sauce
⅛ teaspoon ground Sichuan
peppercorns (Szechwan
peppercorns)
2 tablespoons cornstarch
1 cup chicken broth
½ teaspoon Shao-Hsing wine
½ teaspoon white vinegar

Dofu

with

Spicy

Sauce

■Heat wok over high heat for 1 minute. Add peanut oil. With a spatula coat the wok with the oil. When a wisp of white smoke appears, add chili peppers. When peppers turn black, add ginger and garlic. Stir.

■When garlic turns light brown, add chili paste and stir well. Add ground pork, using spatula to break pork into small pieces.

■When pork changes color, add *dofu*. Stir gently to avoid breaking the *dofu* and cook for 2 minutes.

■Make a well in the center of the mixture. Mix the sauce and pour into the wok, covering it quickly with the *dofu* mixture. Gently stir together. When sauce thickens and bubbles, add sesame oil and mix thoroughly. Remove to a serving dish, top with sliced scallions and serve.

Yield: 6 to 8 servings.

3 cakes spiced *dofu* (see note)
6 ounces lean fresh pork

Marinade:
1 tablespoon egg white
1 teaspoon cornstarch
1 teaspoon sesame oil
½ teaspoon white vinegar
½ teaspoon Shao-Hsing wine
    or sherry
½ teaspoon light soy sauce
½ teaspoon sugar
⅛ teaspoon salt
pinch of white pepper

Sauce:
½ teaspoon cornstarch
½ teaspoon sugar
1 teaspoon dark soy sauce
2 tablespoons chicken broth
pinch of white pepper
3 scallions
2½ cups peanut oil
1 teaspoon ginger, minced
1 teaspoon garlic, minced
1 teaspoon Shao-Hsing wine
    or sherry

Shredded Pork with Spicy *Dofu*

■Cut *dofu* into julienne strips and reserve. Combine egg white, cornstarch, sesame oil, white vinegar, ½ teaspoon wine, light soy sauce, sugar, salt and white pepper in a bowl. Cut pork into julienne strips, marinate for 1 hour and reserve. Combine cornstarch, sugar, dark soy sauce, chicken broth, and white pepper and reserve.

■Remove and discard both ends of scallions. Wash, dry, and cut into 1½-inch pieces (quarter white portions lengthwise). Reserve.

■Place peanut oil in wok; heat to 400 degrees (a wisp of white smoke should appear). Place marinated pork into a large strainer and lower into oil. Oil-blanch the pork for 45 seconds to 1 minute, until it changes color, to seal the meat. Remove from oil, drain, reserve. Empty wok of oil; replace 1 tablespoon for stir-frying.

■Raise heat to high again. Add ginger and garlic to wok. When garlic browns add scallions and *dofu*. Stir-fry together for 1½ to 2 minutes. Add pork and mix all ingredients together. Trickle 1 teaspoon of wine around the inside edge of the wok into the mixture. Make a well in the center, stir sauce and pour in. Stir dish continuously until sauce thickens. Remove and serve.

Yield: 4 servings.

Note: Spiced *dofu* can be found in the refrigerated sections of Asian markets. The cakes are about 2 inches square and ½ inch thick. They are made by simmering firm *dofu* in a mixture of soy sauce, sugar, eight-star anise, Shao-Hsing wine and salt. This curd is used only as a cooking ingredient.

全是中國好吃的食物

All China's Creatures

Human beings are omnivores, which means they will eat anything, and the Chinese are consummate omnivores, because they seem to eat everything. A walk through a major street market, such as the one in Guangzhou already described, quickly reveals that there are no limits on what can be caught, killed, cooked, and eaten; whatever is available is used. Food taboos are a luxury that the Chinese may not be able to afford. But more than that, this is a food system that embraces everything and then skillfully embellishes it to make it attractive, edible, and tasty.

It is no accident that the Chinese symbol for "home" involves a pig under a roof, and no accident that the symbol for "good" is a mother and child —the basic mammalian unit, the model for nurturance and of the most intimate and direct kind of feeding.

There is a down-to-earth lust for life and the process of living here that is reflected in the direct and respectful approach to animals and the manner in which they make use of them, such as the yak's utilization for food, for milk, for a day's work in transporting or plowing, for clothing (wool and leather)—and even for companionship. Each animal is a pool of vivacity as well as an event of nature to be celebrated, albeit captured. As we have seen, the Chinese prefer to buy only what is alive—why would anyone willingly purchase a dead fish?—and when one ties a chicken to a bicycle and drives it home for dinner, he or she is aware of having to kill it and that there is a direct and hearty connection between food and nature. No supermarket impersonality; no abstract body parts. The dried smoked pig's face stares you in the face in every Sichuanese market you care to visit. The flattened preserved duck is a recognizable bird, not a plastic-shiny packaged sculpture. Irritated, squealing pigs are carried on carts through the streets, and their destiny is obvious to every diner.

This is a food chain that has remained visible. There is no hidden link, no secret kept from children and well-bred folk. If the clear-cut carcasses hanging from hooks on stalls in the street are not particularly pretty or perhaps as clean as they could be, there is nonetheless an honesty about the whole matter and a familiarity with nature, rather than its evasion. In a curious but tangible way, eating animals becomes less controversial. There is no guilt by dissociation. The intrusive predatory reality of human life must be shared by everyone. No one has the privilege of petty evasive ignorance. 福

These water buffalo have been brought to graze in these harvested rice fields near the Stone Forest of Yunnan province.

Two young pigs on their way to be sold at the free market in Guilin. They are being chauffeured by a young girl on the back of her bicycle. Pork is the main meat of China.

The tombs of the fifteenth-century Jinjiang kings are less than twenty miles from Guilin. Stone sculptures of people and animals have brooded reclusively for centuries. The area was opened for visitors in 1985.

Dried pork skin hanging in a shop in Chengdu. The skin will puff up when fried, and be served in soup.

Deep-fried birds from Kunming. Such extravagant treats are now available in markets that formerly focused on the more mundane staples of daily life.

Roasted peanuts and fried grasshoppers, a frivolous hors d'oeuvre and snack with drinks. The grasshoppers are a Yunnan specialty and were bought from a huge sack of thousands in the Kunming market.

Dried and flattened ducks,
which are special to
Guangdong province. The
bones remain in the bird,
which is often used for making soup.

Ducks are bred in different
sizes, shapes, and colors
throughout China. This is a
group of Peking ducks on
their march to destiny.

Shanghai Wine Chicken

1 3½ pound chicken, freshly
   killed, washed, fat and
   membranes removed

Marinade:
3 tablespoons Shao-Hsing
   wine
1½ teaspoons salt
¼ teaspoon white pepper
2 tablespoons chicken broth

■Place chicken in a large pot (an aluminum dutch oven preferred). Cover chicken with water and bring to a boil.

■Lower heat, cover pot leaving slight opening, and allow chicken to simmer for about 30 minutes. Turn off heat.

■Remove chicken, drain and set aside to cool.

■When chicken has cooled, chop into pieces 2 inches by 1 inch (skin and bones included). Place on a serving dish.

■Pour marinade over chicken, allow to marinate for 1 hour. Then serve at room temperature.

Yield: 4 to 6 servings.

Peking

Beef

1 pound London broil, sliced
   into pieces 2 inches by
   ½ inch

Marinade:
1 egg white, beaten
1½ teaspoons Shao-Hsing
   wine
1 teaspoon dark soy sauce
2 teaspoons cornstarch
2 teaspoons peanut oil
pinch of white pepper

4 cups peanut oil
1 teaspoon ginger, minced
2 cups scallions, cut into
   2-inch pieces

Sauce:
1½ teaspoons sugar
1½ teaspoons Shao-Hsing
   wine
1 teaspoon white vinegar
1 tablespoon dark soy sauce
1 tablespoon light soy sauce
1 tablespoon hoisin sauce
¼ teaspoon salt
pinch of white pepper
2 teaspoons cornstarch
3 tablespoons chicken broth

1 teaspoon sesame oil

■Marinate beef, refrigerated, for ½ hour.

■Heat oil in wok over high heat to 375 degrees, or until you
see a wisp of white smoke. Add beef and stir until pieces separate and beef loses pink color.

■Drain beef. Drain oil, leaving 2 tablespoons in wok. Turn
heat up high. Add ginger and scallions and stir for 10 sconds.

■Add beef to wok, mix. Make a well, stir sauce and pour. Mix
thoroughly until sauce thickens and changes color. Add sesame
oil, mix well, and serve immediately.

Yield: 4 to 6 servings.

Marinated Spare Ribs

1 rack of ribs, approximately 3 to 3½ pounds. Remove the flap and extra fat from the ribs, then score all over with a sharp knife.

Mix the following ingredients in a bowl:
2 tablespoons oyster sauce
2 tablespoons hoisin sauce
2 tablespoons light soy sauce
2 tablespoons dark soy sauce
2 tablespoons honey
1½ tablespoons brandy or blended whiskey
¾ teaspoon salt
pinch of white pepper

■Line baking pan with foil, lay rack of ribs inside. Using hands, rub the mixture into the rack. The ribs must marinate for at least 4 hours. You may prepare them overnight and marinate them in the refrigerator, but they must be at room temperature at the time of cooking.

■Preheat oven 15 to 20 minutes. Broil ribs for approximately 30 to 50 minutes. You may have to add water if the sauce begins to evaporate. During the broiling process baste the ribs several times and turn rack over several times as well.

Yield: 4 to 6 servings

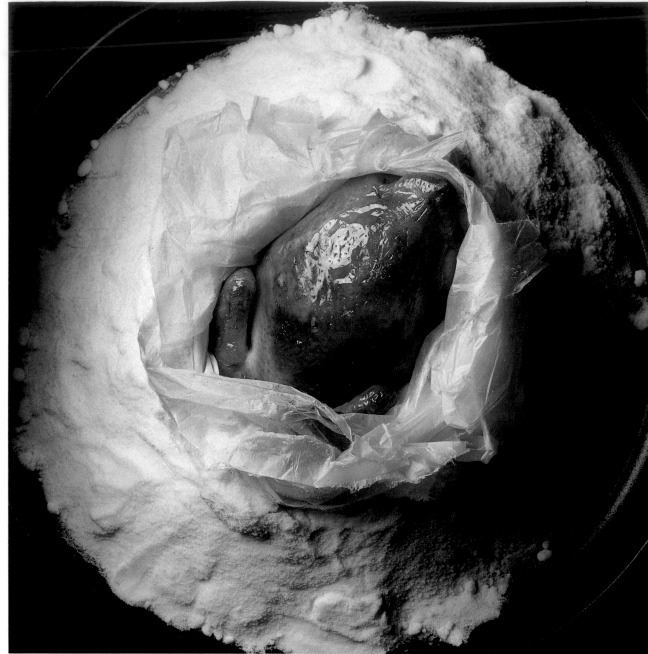

Dried ducks and ducks' legs, in a shop in southern China. Drying is one of the most popular ways of preserving food in China.

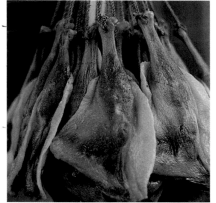

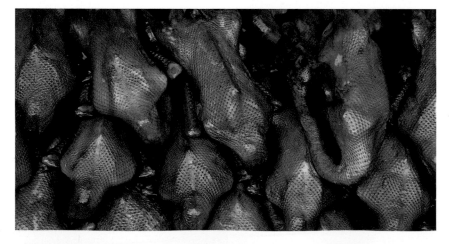

This chicken is wrapped in rice paper and then entirely covered with salt. The packing doesn't make the dish salty—it intensifies the flavor of the meat.

Kebab, shashlik, a specialty of Muslims in the northwest of China.

A suckling pig, a typical part of a wedding feast in southern China. This photo was taken in Guangzhou. Red symbolizes happiness in China.

Peking duck. The bird is brought to the table, the waiter carves off the crisp skin and separates the meat from the carcass, which is then returned to the kitchen for making duck soup.

Peking duck fixings. Wheat-flour pancakes. A thick, sweetish sauce from soybeans, and scallions, which seem especially assertive in China.

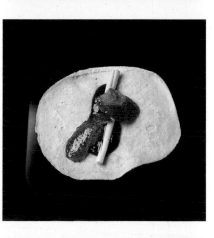

Skin or meat or both, a dab of sauce, and a scallion are placed on a pancake . . .

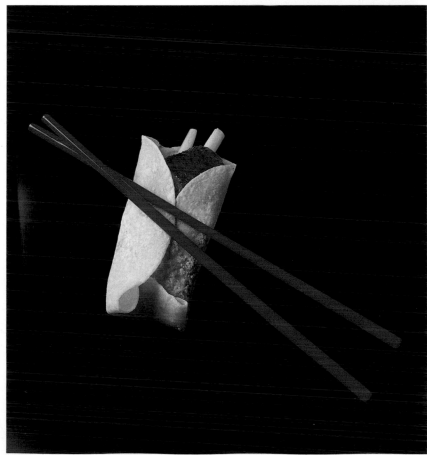

. . . rolled up, and eaten.

These smoked ducks were from the Kunming market and are a specialty of Chongqing, in Sichuan. The men selling them had traveled in a train 1,100 kilometers, over twenty-six hours, to bring these exotic dusky birds to this receptive market.

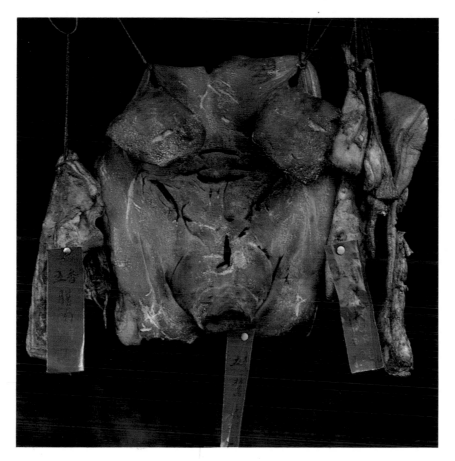

A flattened, dried, and smoked pig's head. Sometimes jam is rubbed over pork before it is smoked. This preparation was seen only in the Chengdu region of Sichuan.

全是中國好的飲料

And All China's Wet Creatures

If nature had feelings, how would it respond to what people did to it? Would it be alarmed or exhilarated by the Great Pyramids, or the eighty-three-story-high dam at Iguacu Falls on the border of Brazil and Paraguay? What would nature feel looking up at the Eiffel Tower? I ask because when I first saw the Great Buddha of Leshan, through an early-morning river mist, I wondered about the response of the rivers it was built to discipline over a thousand years ago, in the hope that the Buddha would make the dangerous rushing waters safer and full of good fish. I ask because even though, like every other fortunate traveler, I have grown rich with tourist memories and therefore less fiercely needy of each new treasure, I was powerfully excited when I first came upon the Buddha, as my ferryboat approached its gigantic base. There, high up, was its benignly haunting face. What effect did it have on fresh running water and on fish?

Presumably none on the water or fish but a marked one on those who built it and those who now come to visit. It describes without ambiguity the importance of rivers and water in China, and underlines the depth and intricacy of the connection between the water and the people. Not far from the looming stone icon is the Dujiangyan irrigation system, which has been in business since 250 B.C.—it is one of the oldest in China— and is an ingenious piece of hydraulic engineering that helped create the neighboring valleys and the most fertile area of China.

This is impressive as far as New World time scales go and also eases us into the older-than-the-hills antiquity of the aquatic scheme. One reason some water creatures appear such bizarre, nightmarish creatures is that they are simply so primitive, so remote from our own evolution, that it is difficult to feel the same sympathy for them that deer or the furry mammals with our kind of legs and arms so easily inspire. For example, the crustaceans look so improbable; think of the lobster, with its awkward jagged physique. But human beings have always chosen to live near water, and we continue to enjoy it—every summer, on every beach, we give up money and privacy for the memory of ancient oceans. We also relish the consumption of their creatures.

The Chinese are no exception in enjoying the food of the sea, rivers, and lakes. They will cook everything they can, every which way, principally by steaming, which is the most common form of basic cooking, and then embellishing with the sauces and assorted garnishes that are one reason for the four or five hundred different dishes offered on the menus of some restaurants. As already noted, the Chinese far prefer to buy live fish, which can command as much as ten times the price of dead ones; or they will buy it dried and perhaps salted, that preservation technique common before Frigidaire. And given the Chinese enthusiasm for lively wet creatures, the marketplace hosts many amateur marine biologists, each of whom boasts some personal technique for jabbing or

tweaking or alarming a fish to assess the vigor of its response and hence its freshness and good health. Little does the especially spirited fish or crab appreciate how poorly served it is by its energy; if it is also good-looking, it is the first victim every time.

Irrigation has had an understandably profound impact on China, in part because everyone had to share water and thus could not completely own their own farms; hence

the basis for Chinese communalism and the apparent need for an overriding administrative system. But the water has also been tamed for its own fertility, not only for the soil's. Chinese fish-farming (or aquaculture) puts to shame the comparatively negligible and inept efforts of Europe and the United States, whose major solution to the problem of fresh fish has been the freezer rather than the neighborhood lake. The Chinese fish farms' inhabitants are specially bred for speed of growth and bonelessness; some carp are so large and yet evidently so small-boned that it seems a wonder they manage to live at all.

The fishfarm is intriguing; it is such a mysterious and quiet form of factory. What *is* the assembly line doing down there? Eventually we find out, over dinner. For example, in that wonderfully shaped dish called Chrysanthemum Fish that we were served after a meal of local specialties at the excellent Dongfeng restaurant in Chengdu: a plump swimmer twisted and seemingly carved to resemble a flower . . . a flower in a complex lemony mild-fire sauce. 福

Natural fishing with a slight, significant twist. The cormorant has a ribbon around its neck, which prevents it from swallowing the fish it has been trained to catch. Teaching the bird can take from three to five years, and one bird can easily feed a family and more. It can catch about twenty to thirty pounds of fish a day. Sometimes two birds will retrieve a fish too heavy for one.

Cormorants cost more than a water buffalo and live for twenty-five years. Paintings from the Tang Dynasty in the seventh century, A.D. show this kind of cormorant enterprise.

River prawns for dinner. The nets are pushed into the mud, shaken, and raised with their crop.

Fishing in Lake Taihu,
near Wuxi, where the fishermen must wait for fish to
enter their system of nets.

Nets and boats on Lake
Taihu.

The Great Buddha of
Leshan. It is the largest seat-
ed Buddha in the world. An
entire soccer team can stand
on its big toe. It was built to
spare fishermen and travelers
from the surging waters flow-
ing together from three
rivers.

An endless fishpond land-
scape near Suzhou. The
ponds are also "streets" used
by boats for travel and
transport. Man-made ponds
ensure fresh fish on
demand in the interior.
The fishermen can clear
each pond of fish with
one huge net.

Dried squid in a shop in
southern China.

Crabs from the market,
where they are tied with a
straw twine. Before they
are cooked they are blackish
green, and afterward a
rather vivid orange.

More squid from Guangzhou.

Emptying a fishpond near Wuxi in the province of Jiangsu.

Dried fish common to southern China.

Shanghai fish.

Eels are often deep-fried, and served with a sweetish sauce.

These tiny fish are a specialty from Lake Taihu in Jiangsu province.

An extravagant seafood collage of shark's fin, cockles, and abalone. Abalone can cost twenty dollars per piece.

Sea cucumber and abalone— banquet fare for a special occasion.

Peking

Sweet

and

Sour

Crispy

Fish

For this typical dish of Peking with the sweetness and sourness favored by the people of the north, a sea bass, a striped bass or a flounder may be used. Their firm flesh is complemented by the sauce.

1 fish, about 2 pounds. Wash, remove membranes, dry with paper towels. Make 4 cuts on each side of the body. Place fish on a large dish and reserve.

Marinade:
1½ tablespoons white wine
1 teaspoon salt
1 teaspoon white vinegar
pinch of white pepper

2 tablespoons pine nuts
6 cups peanut oil
1 egg, beaten
¾ cup cornstarch
½ cup onions, cut into ¼-inch dice
2 teaspoons minced ginger
2 teaspoons minced garlic

Sauce:
⅓ cup sugar
⅓ cup red wine vinegar
¼ teaspoon salt
3 tablespoons catsup
1½ teaspoons dark soy sauce
1 teaspoon sesame oil
3 tablespoons cornstarch
1 teaspoon Shao-Hsing wine or sherry
pinch of white pepper
¾ cup chicken broth

2 scallions, washed, dried, both ends discarded, sliced finely
10 sprigs coriander

■Pour marinade over fish and use hands to rub it in, coating the fish evenly. Let it sit for 15 minutes.

■Heat wok over high heat for 1 minute, add peanut oil. When a wisp of white smoke appears, lower pine nuts in a fine net strainer into the oil for 10 seconds. Then remove from heat, drain and set aside.

■Spread cornstarch on a sheet of waxed paper. Coat fish with beaten egg and place on cornstarch. Coat the body thoroughly with cornstarch, including the cuts in the skin. Shake off excess cornstarch.

■Reheat oil over high heat. When a wisp of white smoke appears, place coated fish in a Chinese strainer and lower it into the oil. Deep-fry for 10 minutes, until fish browns. Tip the fish's tail and head into the oil if it is too large, to ensure that it will be fully cooked. If needed, a ladle can be used to pour hot oil over these portions of the fish. When the fish is brown and crisp, remove from oil and allow to drain in a strainer over a bowl.

■Pour oil from the wok. Wipe with a paper towel. Replace 2 tablespoons of oil in the wok and heat. Stir-fry onions for 4 to 5 minutes, until they become golden brown. Add ginger and garlic and stir together for about 45 seconds. Stir the sauce and pour into the wok. Mix all ingredients thoroughly until the sauce becomes thick and begins to bubble.

■Place fish on a preheated platter, pour the sauce over it. Sprinkle with pine nuts and scallions, garnish with coriander and serve immediately.

Yield: 6 to 8 servings.

Chopped Shrimps Sichuan

1 pound shrimps (shelled,
  deveined, dried thoroughly
  and cut into sections)
½ cup shallots, cubed
1 to 2 fresh hot peppers,
  cut across into thin rounds
¾ cup sweet green peppers,
  cubed
¾ cup sweet red peppers,
  cubed
4 cloves of garlic, minced
1 tablespoon brown bean
  sauce
1 tablespoon white wine

Sauce:
2 tablespoons catsup
¾ teaspoon salt
2 teaspoons sugar
1 teaspoon white vinegar
pinch of white pepper
1 teaspoon sesame oil
1½ teaspoons cornstarch
2 tablespoons chicken broth

4½ tablespoons peanut oil
10 lettuce leaves, washed and
  dried

■Heat wok over high heat for 1 minute, then place 1½ tablespoons of peanut oil in wok and coat wok with oil. Brown the peppers for 1 minute, then remove from wok. Wash wok and spatula.

■Heat wok, add 3 tablespoons peanut oil. Brown shallots for 30 seconds, add minced garlic and mix together for 1 minute.

■Add brown bean sauce, stir. Add shrimp, spread in a thin layer. When they turn pink, turn them over. Add white wine around edges of the wok, then mix thoroughly.

■Add peppers and mix together. Make a well in center of mixture, stir sauce and pour into well. Mix thoroughly.

■Serve shrimp in individual lettuce leaves. Roll leaves around shrimp.

Yield: 4 to 6 servings.

Heng

Yang

Spicy

Scallops

1 pound scallops (sliced)
½ red pepper (diced)
½ green pepper (diced)
6 water chestnuts (sliced)
1½ teaspoons cloud ears
   (soak in hot water for
   ½ hour)
3 tablespoons chopped
   scallions
1 teaspoon minced ginger
½ teaspoon minced garlic
2 cups peanut oil

Sauce:
3 tablespoons soy sauce
⅛ teaspoon white pepper
1 teaspoon sugar
½ teaspoon salt
2 tablespoons Shao-Hsing
   wine
1 teaspoon vinegar
¼ cup chicken broth
½ teaspoon chili paste
1 teaspoon hoisin sauce
1 teaspoon sesame oil
1 teaspoon cornstarch mixed
   with 2 teaspoons water to
   form a paste

■Heat wok. Add oil. Heat to about 350 degrees. Add scallops, peppers, water chestnuts and cloud ears and stir-fry for 2 minutes. Drain ingredients and oil. Leave 3 tablespoons oil in wok.

■Turn heat up high. Add garlic, ginger, scallions. Stir 3 times and add sauce ingredients. Bring to a boil. Add scallops and vegetables. Bring to a boil again. Quickly stir cornstarch paste, and slowly add, while stirring, until desired thickness is achieved.

Yield: 2 servings.

Shrimp

in

the

Style

of

Peking

1 pound large shrimps
3 tablespoons peanut oil
1 tablespoon minced garlic
1½ teaspoons minced garlic
1 tablespoon Shao-Hsing wine

Sauce:
2 teaspoons sugar
½ teaspoon salt
1 teaspoon white vinegar
1 teaspoon dark soy sauce
2 tablespoons catsup
1½ teaspoons cornstarch
pinch of white pepper
1¼ cups chicken broth

1 tablespoon sesame oil
2 tablespoons white portions
  of leeks shredded

■Using a small pointed shears, cut along back of shrimp along vein line. Open shrimp slightly with fingers under running water and remove vein. Drain excess water, dry thoroughly with paper towel. Cut shrimp in half, across. Repeat with all shrimp.

■Heat wok over high heat for 1 minute. Add peanut oil, coat wok sides with spatula. When white smoke appears add minced ginger and garlic.

■When garlic turns light brown add shrimp. Spread in a thin layer, and tip wok from side to side to make certain all shrimp are cooked. When they turn pink on the bottom, turn them over, and mix with ginger and garlic.

■Add wine around edge of wok, stir. Make a well in center of mixture, stir sauce, pour into well. Mix thoroughly. When sauce thickens add sesame oil and shredded leeks. Mix well, remove from heat and serve immediately.

Yield: 4 to 6 servings.

Squid fried in oil. Squid is a common dish, boiled or fried, all over China. It's almost always cut in this unusual pattern.

醫藥食物

Medicine

Food

While some modern Euro-American men feel powerful when they mount on their den walls the head of a deer with dramatic antlers, many Chinese men evidently feel powerful and potent if they can *consume* shavings or extracts of the antlers. This is part of a central and highly consequential aspect of Chinese eating: the use of food as if it were medicine and of medicine as if it were food.

It is also a highly complex matter, involving elaborate botanical knowledge and physiological theory and, of course, an understanding of the broad role of herbal medicine and its related arts and sciences in the health practices of Chinese people throughout history. How can the uninitiated begin to comprehend the meaning of a list of specialties confidently given by a Sichuan pharmacy: "caterpillar fungus, the tuber of elevated gastrodia, the bark of eucommia, the bulb of fritallary, Coptis, the rhizome of chuanziong, tremella, ginseng, northeast China antler, pseudo-ginseng, root codonopsis (dangshen), Chinese angelica, Poris cocoa, cemdiobii minima and pearls as well as prepared medicines, tonics and medicated liquors."

Is the ultimate impact of consuming varying amounts of such substances and avoiding others equivalent to the Western belief in the importance of vitamins C and D and the dangers of cholesterol, in the value of some roughage in the diet and the undesirability of foods relying principally on sugar for their calories? Is the medicine similar to acupuncture, which appears to work when performed by competent practitioners but for reasons not wholly clear to Western scientists? There must be an empirical basis to it all, in that it has persisted for over two thousand years and thus can be presumed to boast some tested connection to the facts of life. It is true that the increase in the life expectancy of the Chinese people has been dramatic—almost thirty years—since the Liberation in 1949; some or even much of this may be due to the adoption of Western medical techniques, better control of communicable diseases, more immediate and effective treatment of infant illnesses, and so on. Nevertheless, there remains in

China a durable commitment among the population at large to forms of traditional medicine for particular kinds of illness. And its "Four Modernizations" notwithstanding, the Chinese government is actively promoting not only the recording of traditional medical practices but also the extension of their use where appropriate. There is no way of appreciating China's food without an understanding of its relationship to feeling bad and getting better.

The visitor can get a sense of the connection of food and medicine from a glance at the prescription-filling room of a Chinese pharmacy, which looks rather like a kitchen: the personnel wear hats, and the "ingredients" for a particular remedy are assembled just as Chinese dishes are, to be triumphantly integrated in the last moments before serving. I had the same impression in a Shanghai fish-canning factory, which produced canned fish for export and also made cod-liver oil and vitamins out of the fish oil. It seemed wholly reasonable to the managers of the pharmacy that there should be a direct connection between food and medicine. And indeed, the golden glycerine pills piled along the assembly table near a sunny window looked for all the world like giant versions of the yellow California caviar so prized by those who not only savor caviar but seek it out in unusually intriguing forms.

Certainly there is a sense of the role of nature in Chinese society that is directly amenable to the use of herbal and other traditional medicines. It recalls one of these tiny highly revealing facts I acquired in the market in Leshan, where I asked about several blind people being guided into what appeared to be a shop, and was told that they worked as masseurs! A form of karate, this—use the strength of your deficit to create an advantage. In the same way, food-in-nature helps man-in-nature, for example in the very important matter of balancing spiritual "heat" and spiritual "coolness." Unlike Western ideas of food as private ingredients of a healthy individual life, or the Indian idea so tied to the caste structure of food as an index of spiritual place, the Chinese regard food as a natural summary of social and personal forces. That is why it is possible to eat antidotally or aggressively, to forestall specific diseases and problems or cure them. Just as no meal or snack or simple drink is without some social significance and probably social contact, so foods are reckoned to have some broader significance than just their own existence. No food is just the food it is. 福

"Recipes" for medicine, freshly made to order each morning, follow the doctor's prescription. The white-clad pharmacists mix medicines the way cooks prepare food: fresh every day, following the individual recipes. A prescription may change as often as every day.

Evidently to stimulate their potency, some elderly Chinese men drink the blood of snakes, drained into a cocktail glass.

A mixture of herbal medicines in a drugstore in Beijing.

Two separate herbs, shown together, are both supposed to attack "the insects of the stomach."

A street-side herb shop on the free market street in Kunming, Yunnan province. The framed sign is a license to sell.

Factory-produced, plastic-clad health soups. They take several hours to cook in the factory, and thirty minutes or so at home. Ingredients: Imperatac, sugar cane, water chestnut slices, carrot slices. "It is an ideal soup mix suitable for all ages, *et. al.*," says the package.

Water shields grown in Lake Taihu. These vegetables are considered very health-giving, particularly beneficial to the lungs and to fight high blood pressure.

Deer antlers at a deer farm near Beijing. Once a year, the horns are cut and air-dried. In drugstores, thin slices are sold. Or the horns may be boiled and the essence sold as pills or drops.

A deer whose horns had been removed a month before. Young deer are the most prized and considered the most efficacious.

Deer antler slices, very expensive and thought to help prolong life—the deer is said to be the only animal able to find the sacred fungus of immortality. Deerhorn is supposed to stimulate men's potency and strengthen women's breasts.

到市場去

To Market, to Market

到市場去

The Zoo in Chengdu boasts twelve giant panda bears, the largest collection anywhere, and most visitors go to see them. The reason for the worldwide interest in the animals is clear right away; there is something elementally appealing about their faces, their tubby bodies, the unthreatening way they move, and of course their fate as the living embodiment of an archetypical toy. The species is an endangered one, both because of the evident sexual fastidiousness of the bears and their reclusive tendencies, and the fact that they eat mainly a certain bamboo that flowers infrequently, so sometimes their diet is "shut down." The single most charming image I have of the pandas is of the delicate, almost formal manner in which an adult male sat, quietly holding a sheaf of bamboo shoots and occasionally slipping some into his mouth, like a child enjoying licorice, or as precisely as a gourmet savoring a young carrot of the new season.

Animals and fish are "available" all year long, but fruits and vegetables are seasonal and generally have a limited useful period once they are harvested. They must be fresh or they must be preserved. They come to market each day compelled by the force of nature. So any marketplace is a revealing pageant of a society's ongoing agricultural advances. And no more so than in contemporary China, where the sumptuous variety to be found daily in the free markets of the cities, towns, and villages reflects tangibly the impact of the government's shift of emphasis from collective farming to a mixture of collective and individual, family agriculture. The settlements once called communes are now known as townships, and the semantic difference is a significant one. Not only has productivity increased enormously, but the markets have become highly sensitive to what diners want, and the quality and variety of produce and dairy reflects this.

This is nothing new, just a return to the older patterns of growing food of which Chinese cuisine has always been the elegant evidence. Any visitor there must be struck by the sense of pleasure, almost of wonder, inhabitants seem to take in their recent deliverance from the austere heyday of high ideology, when pleasures were meted out by bureaucrats and when the streets were evidently reserved for the earnest transport of goods and services–when production was the Chinese king and consumption a foreign devil. Now it is possible to see daily, on the way to work, the literal fruits and other expressions of human involvement with fertile nature.

As with all liberties of the sensibility their loss is more stunning than the losers expect and their return is like an obviously overdue spring. And in China you can taste it. 福

Picking water chestnuts in a pond near Yixing, in the Jiangsu province. The boat also serves as a storage bin for the chestnuts.

Chestnuts are widely used in China and their aroma when they are roasting enhances many a market. However, these are red water chestnuts, which are never roasted. Two are real and one was made of sticky rice at the Nanlin restaurant in Suzhou.

170   Which is which?

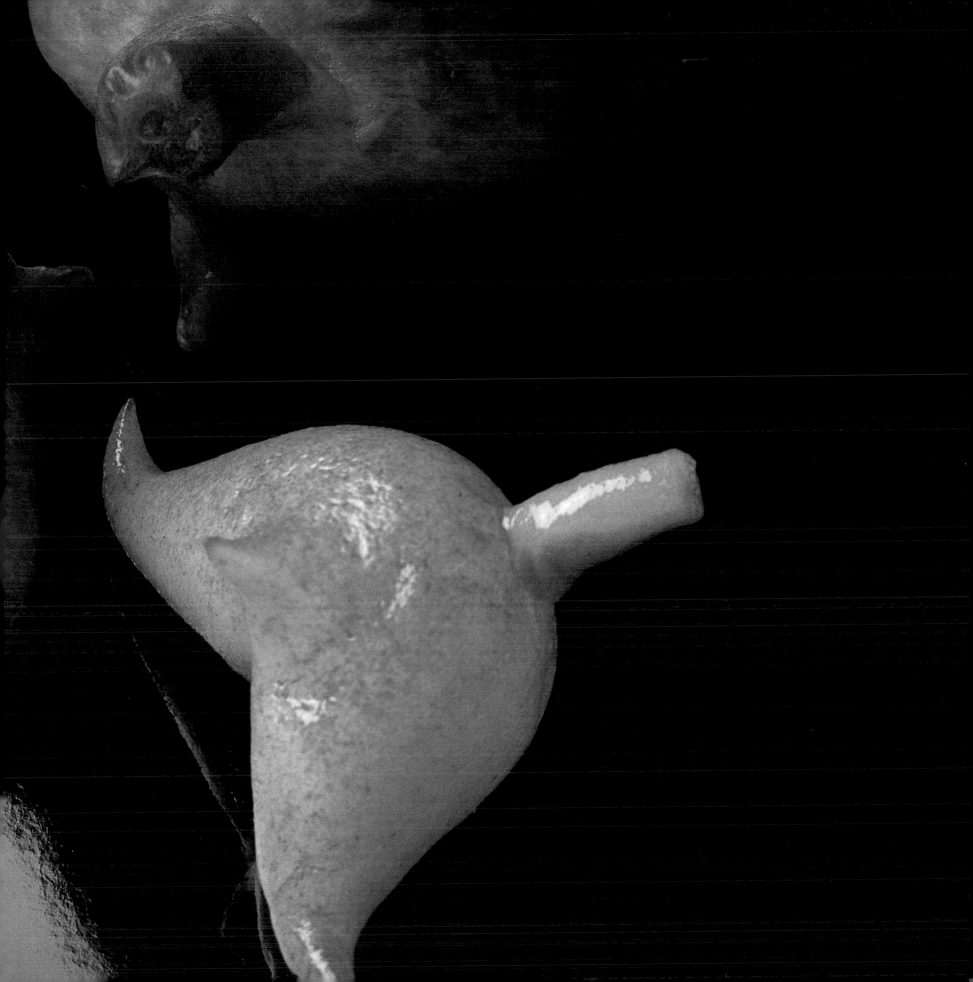

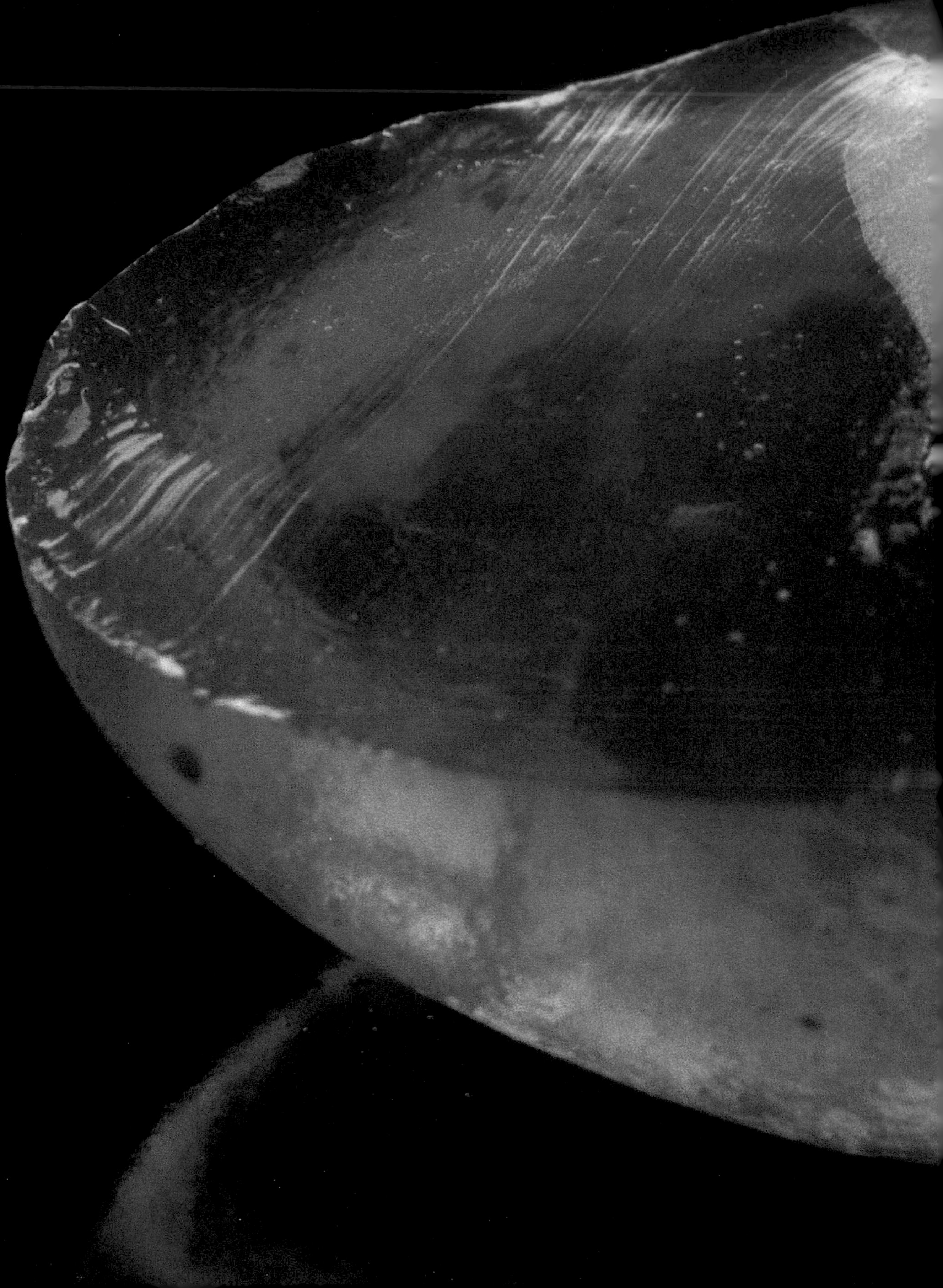

A preserved chicken egg
sold in markets and restaurants all over China. Fresh
eggs are dipped into a mixture of lime, salt, ash, sea-
soning, soda, and tea. Stored
in a clay pot, the eggs will
still be edible six months
later.

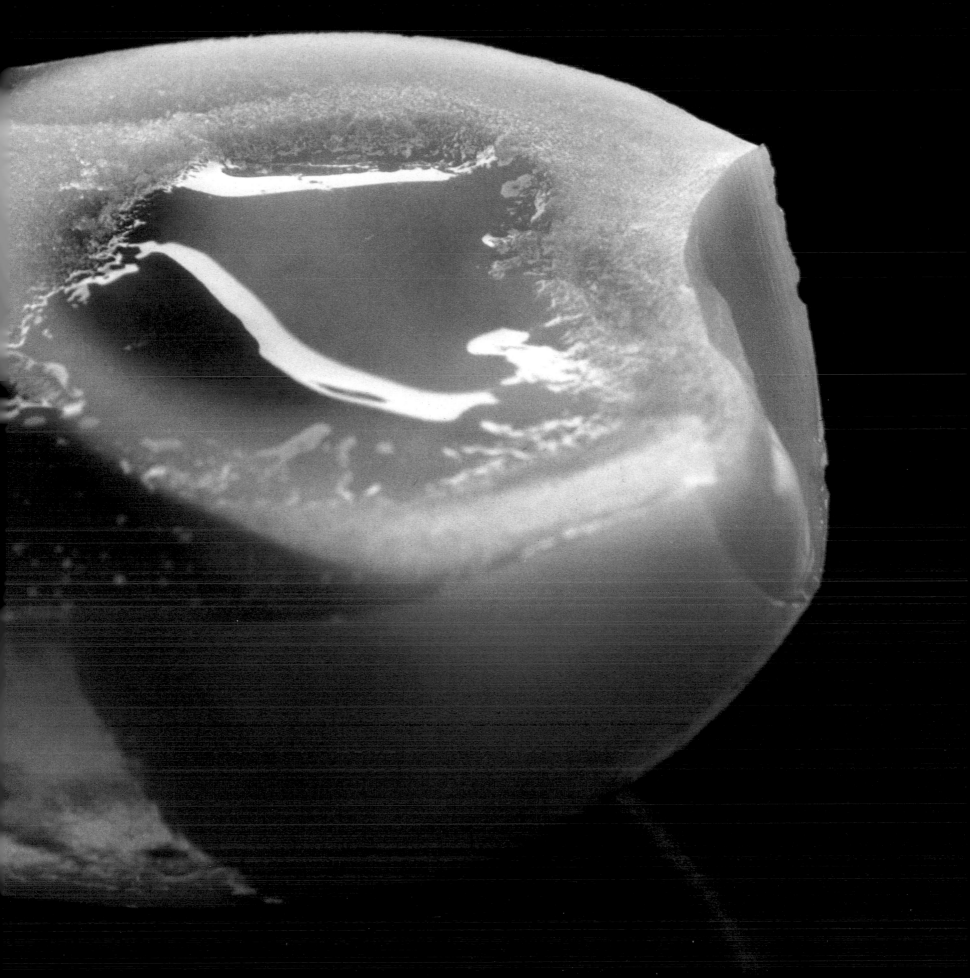

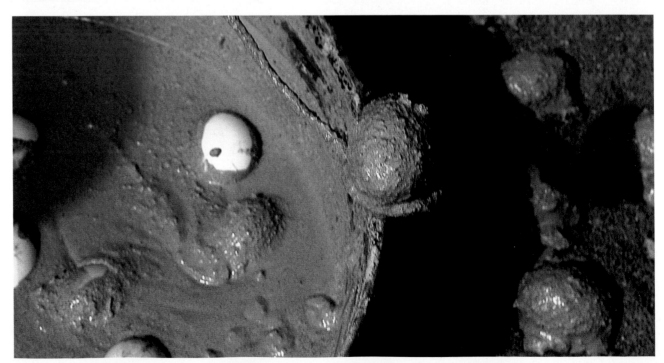

Stages of the process of
preserving eggs.

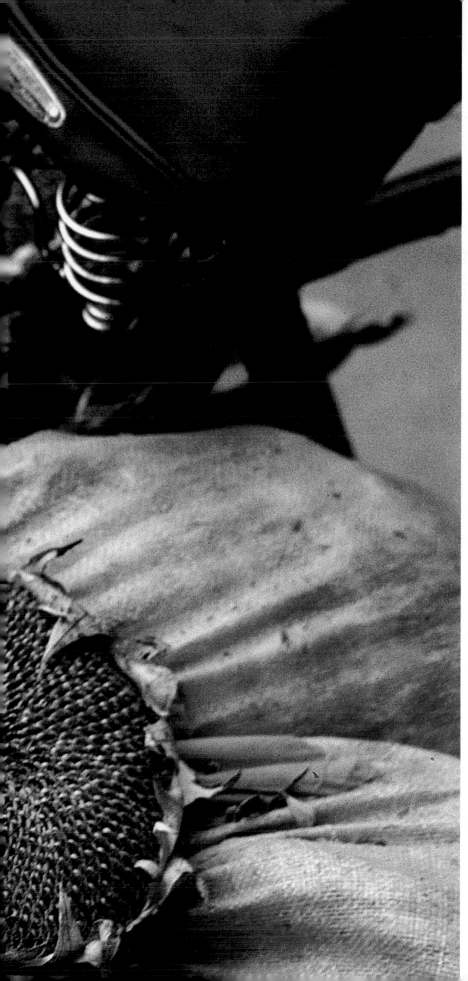

Dried sunflowers on a bicycle in the Lanzhou market. They are popular in movie theaters, and children eat them in the street.

Garlic, garlic, garlic. Here
preserved in a thick soy sauce
made in Yunnan. Yet
another method of using this
omnipresent vegetable,
which is thought to prolong
life.

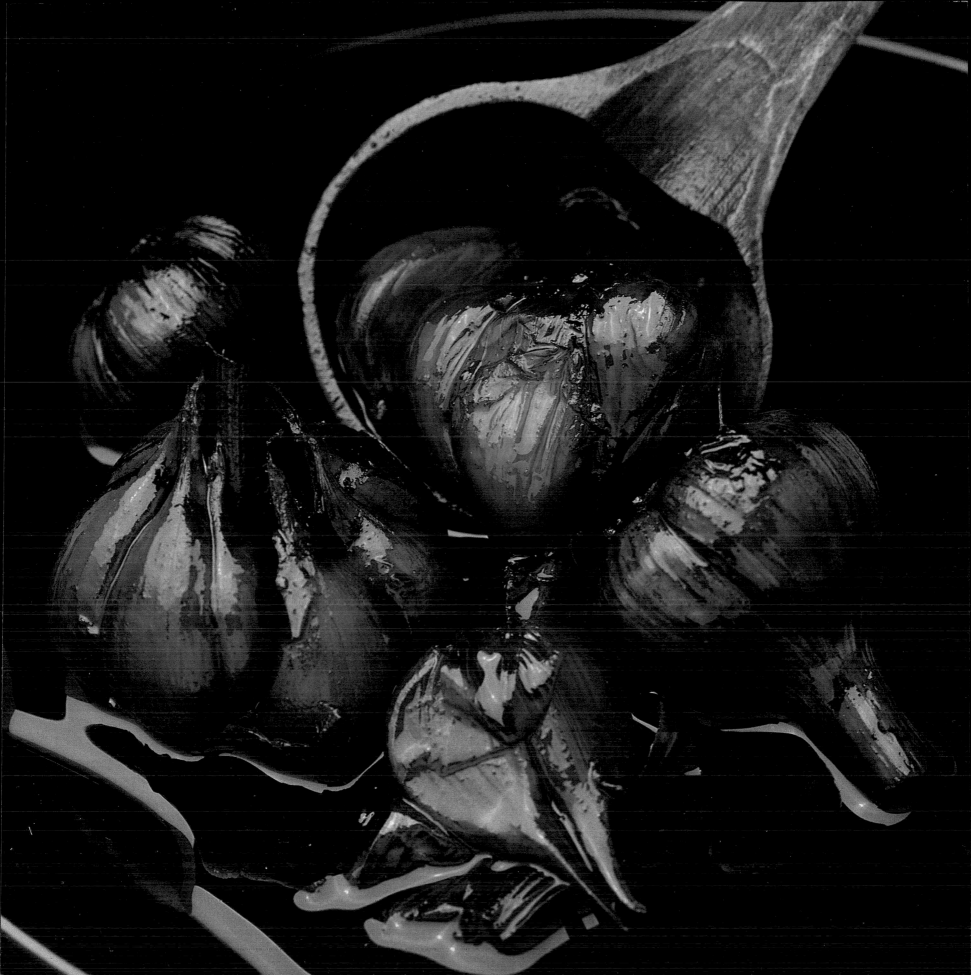

A pottery factory in Yixing. The product is used mainly for preserving food. The pots are stacked up in unimaginable numbers.

Pixian chili paste. When the sun is shining the straw lids are removed to speed the paste on its way to incendiary intensity.

Preserved vegetables for sale in the Kunming market. For breakfast, a few bits are often added to liven up some rice porridge.

Red chilies in the
Chengdu market, and the
characteristic scale of
Chinese markets.

Peppers drying in the sun
of Yunnan.

Red peppers being delivered
to a shop in Lanzhou.

A spinachy vegetable, cheap and abundant in most of China.

Vegetable noodle soup. Broth will be added, and then perhaps soy sauce, or ginger, or hot chili oil, or . . .

For sale, scallions in Shanghai.

Qing cai, a quickly grown vegetable that is widely available. It is often preserved, or cooked simply.

Qing cai can grow in twenty-five days. The hearts are the tenderest, choicest bits.

Red rape, a Sichuanese vegetable.

Chestnuts in the top basket, small onions in the one below. From Sichuan.

Ginger is used everywhere in China. It is supposed to have a warming effect on the body.

Young green beans, some-
what expensive and hence
a luxury.

Purple beans from the Wuxi region.

Green beans.

Roasted beans, often a snack food with alcoholic drinks.

The stem of the wild-rice plant is sold in just this form in many parts of China. It is peeled just before it is given to the customer.

Sugarcane in a Sichuan field.

Raw brown sugar is made in factories and is available in various shapes.

Cane ready for transport.

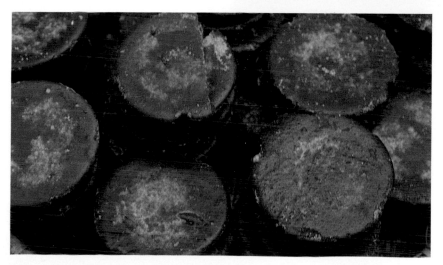

Chinese walnuts enjoy a good reputation in many countries. Near the Stone Forest in Kunming, a government tea house serves its clients walnuts as well as tea. You are given a bunch of walnuts and a wooden hammer. Then you place the nut in a hole carved into a piece of wood and . . . crack! Brilliantly simple, sharply noisy.

Chestnuts are often served with fowl or by themselves, as an appetizer. These were boiled in water together with anise by a farmer who lived some forty-five miles north of Beijing.

The Yunnan province is known for the variety of its mushrooms.

Because pork is so predominant in China, many spices are enlisted to lend special tastes to the meat. This is a selection for sale in a shop of the market of Lanzhou.

An array of dried Chinese mushrooms. These are usually very expensive; much of the crop is exported. The spongy kind at the top of the collection is often eaten in a clear, sweetened soup.

Different varieties of pumpkins and melons from Guangzhou.

Winter melon. This is considered to have a cooling effect on the body.

A bamboo forest near Yixing. Bamboo shoots are eaten. The trees are used for scaffolding on construction sites. Smaller poles are everywhere used across the shoulders to carry things—they are strong and flexible.

Winter bamboo shoots.

What a bamboo shoot looks like when it is sliced open.

Bamboo shoot in Chengdu.

Dried bamboo shoots of Lanzhou. These are soaked in water before cooking.

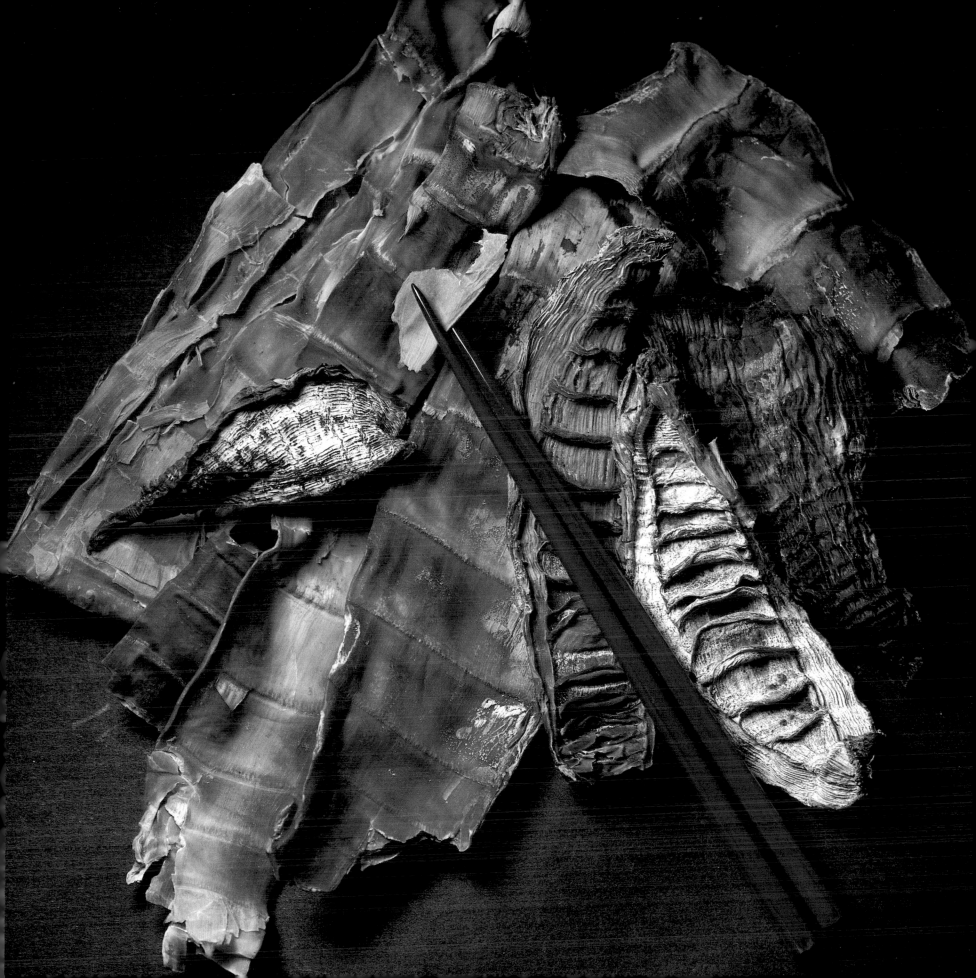

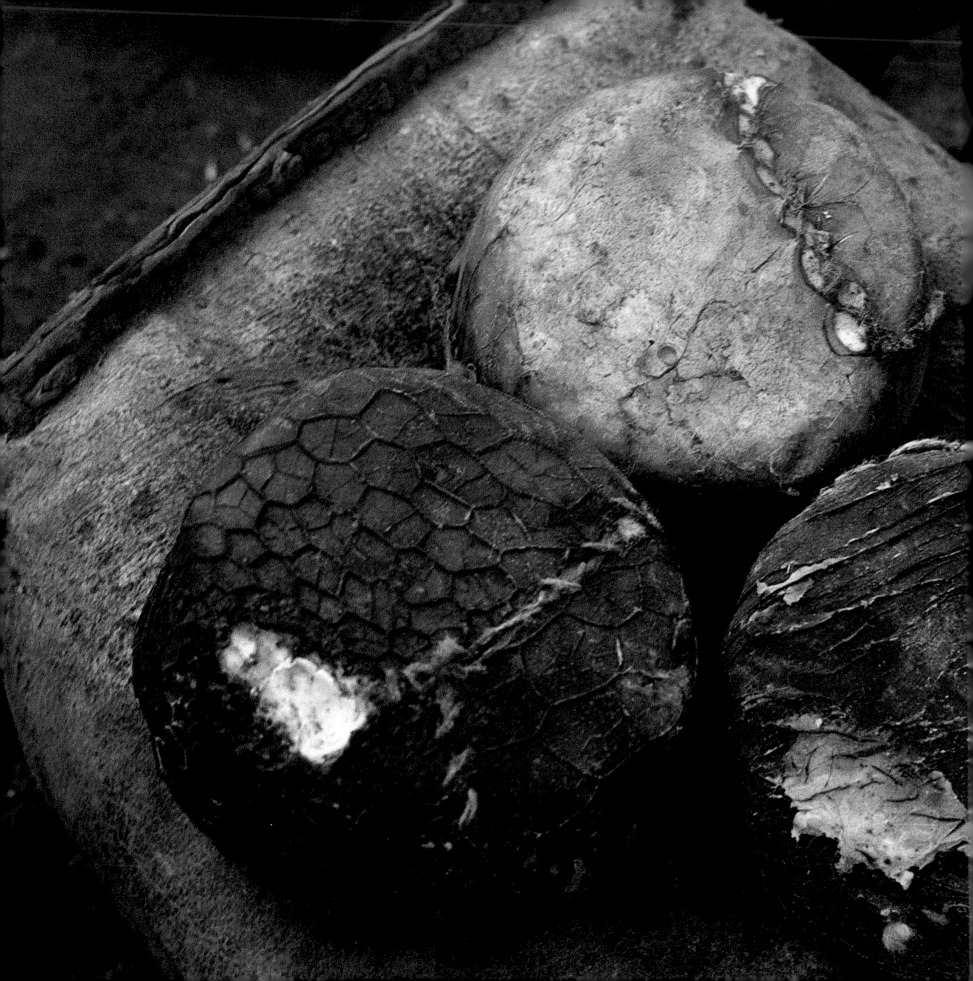

Dried yak cheese on a
string in Lhasa. Tibetans often snack on this stone-
hard cheese, or they mix it
with roasted barley flour
and tea or water and eat it
without further cooking.

Yak butter for sale in Lhasa.
It can be between one and
three years old. The older it
is, the more piquant. It is
very expensive—about two
dollars a pound. It is often
wrapped and stored in sheep
or yak intestine. The
high, dry air of Tibet makes
it necessary to rub one's
skin with some fat—often
yak butter.

Fresh lotus root standing up, dried lotus root lying on its side. Grown everywhere in China except in very dry regions such as Tibet and Mongolia.

A table decoration—the lotus flower made of peas, egg white, cucumber peel, and sliced sausage. A re-creation created by the chef of the Hubin hotel in Wuxi.

Every part of the lotus plant is used, including the root. The lotus is considered sacred and an example to us all, because it grows out of mud but rises above it, is not defiled by it. It is also an emblem of summer fruitfulness.

■Heat wok over high heat, 45 seconds to 1 minute, then add peanut oil, and coat wok with oil using spatula. Add ginger, salt and garlic. When garlic turns light brown, add cabbage and stir. Add carrots, stir and mix. Add bamboo shoots, stir and mix. Add mushrooms, tiger lily buds, cloud ears, and *dofu*, stir and mix. Add scallions, stir and mix.

■Make a well in the center of the vegetable mixture. Stir sauce and pour in the wok. Cover with vegetables, then stir and mix quickly. When sauce thickens and turns dark brown, remove from wok and serve with pancakes.

Yield: 10 servings.

Note: When cooking vegetables in a wok, a bowl of cold water should be kept on hand. If vegetables are too dry, dip hand in water and sprinkle—to create steam to help cook them.

Vegetarian Mushu Pork

2 cups of cabbage, cut into ⅛ x 3-inch lengths

½ cup of carrots, peeled, threaded into ¼ x 2-inch pieces

⅓ cup bamboo shoots, sliced into ⅛ x 2-inch lengths

2 tablespoons cloud ears, washed, soaked and broken up if too large

8 Chinese dried mushrooms, washed, soaked, stems removed, and cut into ⅛-inch strips

48 dried tiger lily buds, soaked in hot water until soft, hard ends removed, and cut in half

8 slices dried *dofu*, soaked in hot water until soft, and cut into ⅛-inch slices

2 scallions, washed, dried, both ends discarded, cut into 1½-inch threads

¾ teaspoon salt

3 tablespoons peanut oil

1 teaspoon minced ginger

1 teaspoon minced garlic

Sauce:

1 teaspoon sugar

2 teaspoons dark soy sauce

1 tablespoon Shao-Hsing wine or sherry

1 tablespoon hoisin sauce

pinch of white pepper

2 teaspoons cornstarch

3 tablespoons water

1 teaspoon sesame oil

Spicy String Beans

12 ounces fresh green string beans: remove both ends, wash, and dry very thoroughly because they are to be blanched in hot oil
3 cups peanut oil
2 teaspoons minced ginger
2 teaspoons minced garlic
2 small fresh red hot peppers, minced

Sauce:
1 teaspoon dark soy sauce
½ teaspoon sugar
½ teaspoon sesame oil
½ teaspoon white vinegar
½ teaspoon Shao-Hsing wine or sherry
1 teaspoon cornstarch
3 tablespoons water
pinch of white pepper

■Heat a wok over high heat for 40 seconds. Add peanut oil. When a wisp of white smoke appears, lower string beans into oil with a Chinese strainer and oil-blanch for 2 minutes, or until beans soften. Remove with strainer and drain over a bowl.

■Pour off oil from wok. Replace 1½ tablespoons of oil in wok. Over high heat add ginger, garlic, and hot peppers, and stir for 45 seconds to 1 minute. Add string beans to wok and stir-fry for 1 minute.

■Make a well in the center of the beans. Stir the sauce, pour in the well. Mix all ingredients thoroughly. When sauce thickens, remove from wok and serve immediately.

Yield: 4 to 6 servings.

Stir-fried Fresh Vegetables

6 fresh water chestnuts,
  peeled, washed, dried,
  sliced into julienne strips
½ cup bamboo shoots,
  julienned
1½ cups snow peas, strings
  removed, washed, dried,
  cut diagonally and
  julienned
1½ cups sweet red peppers,
  washed, dried, seeds
  removed, julienned into
  2-inch-long pieces
1½ cups green peppers,
  prepared as above
2½ tablespoons peanut oil
1 slice fresh ginger
salt to taste

■Heat wok over high heat for about 40 seconds. Add peanut oil and, with spatula, coat sides of the wok. Add ginger and salt to oil.

■The oil is heated when a wisp of white smoke appears. Add the water chestnuts and stir for 30 seconds. Add bamboo shoots and stir, mixing, for another 30 seconds. Add snow peas, mix and stir for an additional 30 seconds.

■Add the red and green peppers and stir all of the ingredients together for 1 to 2 minutes. Remove vegetables from wok, place in a heated dish and serve immediately.

Note: Have a bowl of cold water on hand during the cooking process. If the vegetables are too dry, dip a hand in the bowl of water and flick water into the wok. This creates steam and the vegetables cook well.

Yield: 4 to 6 servings.

Sichuan Pickle Soup with Pork

4 cups chicken broth
3 ounces shredded lean pork
2 ounces Sichuan pickle, shredded (Szechwan pickle)
2 ounces bamboo shoots (shredded)
12 mushrooms, medium (soaked, washed, stems removed, julienned)
1 teaspoon Shao-Hsing wine
1 dash ground pepper
½ teaspoon salt
1 scallion (use white part only, shredded)

Pour chicken broth into soup pot. Bring to boil. Add pork, cabbage, mushrooms, and bamboo shoots and stir. Bring to boil again, add wine, pepper and salt. Stir and bring to boil. Ladle into soup bowl and garnish with scallion.

Yield: 4 to 6 servings

Heat

Everyone knows that an important reason the Chinese cook food cut into small pieces is to save fuel; peoples' time has been less scarce and valuable than wood, coal, oil, or gas. Traditionally the amount of fuel needed to cook something defined how long it would take, as in the instruction to "cook for one bundle of wood." When the wood is burned the food is done. But of course food is prepared every which way, and sometimes a number of methods are used for one dish. Something may be steamed first and then deep-fried, or first boiled and then simmered, then quick-fried in very hot oil. Flavors may be combined at different points in the preparation of a dish; a kind of reconstruction of the different elements occurs and new properties emerge. Different forms of heat applied at different times produce an encyclopedia of tastes, and all the while the diner asks in bafflement, "How *does* the chef do this?" Just by embracing the complexity of heat, along with the complexity of flavor, of texture, of color, of shape.

Some of the cooking techniques are rather showy, as with the Mongolian hot pot perched in the center of the table, into whose broth the diner places a sliver of this or that, dips it into a sauce of this or that, and eats it—a procedure some find boring, with a result to match. Or there is the intrinsically dramatic wok, with its terrifically high heats –"big heat," as it is called– and the often fierce speed of its ardent tossings and turnings, its occasional leap of flame as oil chances into the fire, its huge hisses and crackles, the relatively muscular way the whole procedure is performed, and the unforgivingness such speed and intensity of heat make inevitable. Or there is the quiet force of the brazier, over which is cooked the sliced Mongol lamb; or the clay pot with a spout inside it, which directs steam to chicken and vegetables that start out dry and end up perfect soup. Or the roiling bubbly tubs of hot oil in which street vendors fry their wares, or the little skyscrapers of steaming bamboo baskets with their rolls or buns or dumplings or fillets of fish turned over to the hot mist so important to that style of cuisine.

Or food can be cooked, in a sense, by preserving it. In salt, or with pepper, or by fermentation, or by giving it alcoholic content, or by sealing it in the myriad shapes and sizes of pottery that abound. It can become jam or chutney or jelly or pickle or sauce, or it can be dried in the sun, like noodles. Or, as with the wrongly named thousand-year-old egg, covered in lime and ash and buried for a few weeks. Or, as with "Beggar's Chicken," covered with clay and baked alongside hot stones placed in a hole in the earth—a technique developed, according to legend, by a malefactor who had to stash his loot and cook it without a trace, fuss, or incriminating smoke. A tasty luxury developed out of economic and social necessity. What his countrymen did and are still doing with China's food. 福

The eternal kettle, boiling water for all the tea in China.

Baozi in a high-rise bamboo steamer in Lanzhou.

Rice is steamed in Kunming.

A steam pot soup in Yixing. The food is cooked by steam rising through the spout in the center. This gentle process takes at least four hours and sometimes overnight. The steam condenses and becomes—soup!

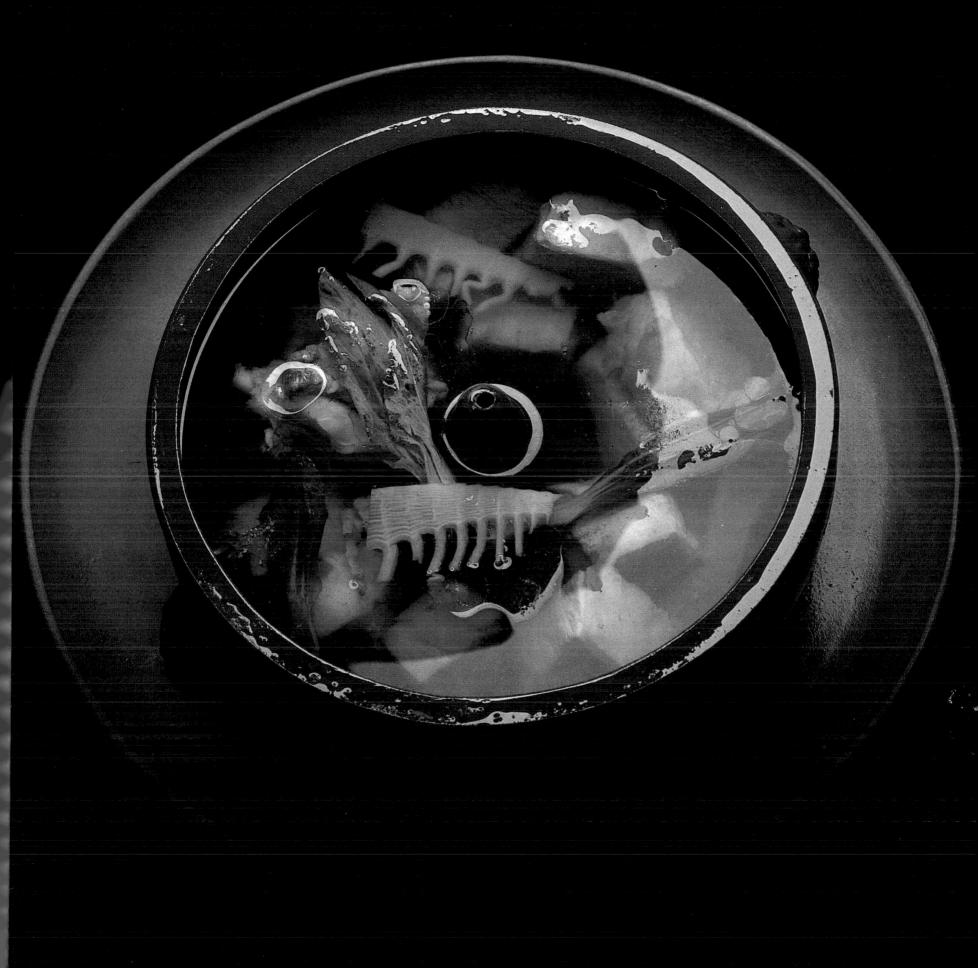

Soup is cooking in a wok,
in the night market of
Kunming.

Beijing duck in a traditional
oven.

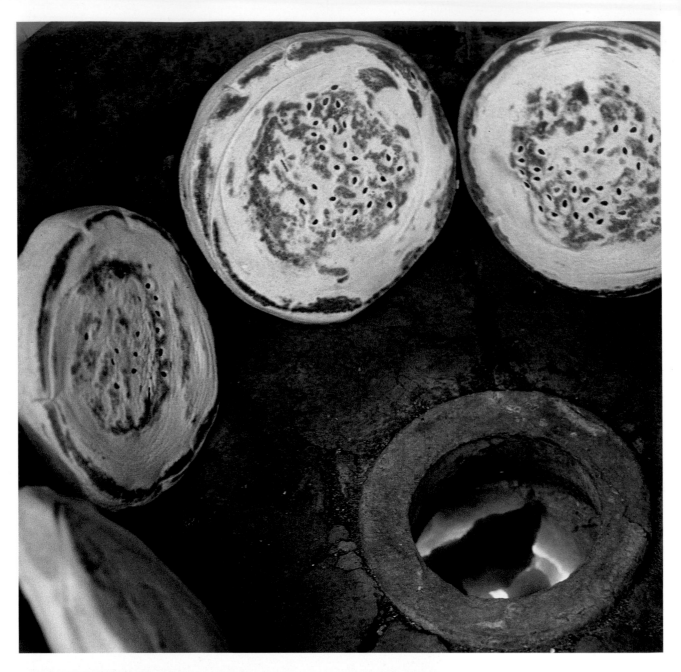

In the Kaorouji restaurant
of Beijing, slices of mutton
are grilled on an iron plate.
This is a Muslim restaurant;
no pork is served.

Rice soup made by Tibetan monks over an open fire in Lhasa.

Sweet potatoes baking in a metal barrel over a charcoal fire.

Sweet potato hot potato.

Noodle soup in a night market.

The Mongolian hot pot is
served in winter only and is a
Beijing favorite. Diners poke
bits of meat, vegetable,
squid—whatever—into a
boiling broth and then into
one of many savory sauces.
It's a very popular family-re-
union dish, always surround-
ed by an animated buzz.

Wheat-flour breads ringing
coals in an oven of the
kitchen of the Evergreen
commune, or township, near
Beijing.

Steamed

Fish

1 2½ pound whole red snap-
per (or striped bass, sea
bass, or flounder), cleaned
thoroughly inside and out,
intestines and extra fat
removed, and the fish
washed inside and out and
dried well.

Sprinkle inside the cavity and
outside with a mixture of:
2 teaspoons salt
2 tablespoons peanut oil
1½ teaspoons sesame oil
2 tablespoons thin soy sauce
1 tablespoon white wine
4 large slices of fresh ginger,
shredded
½ teaspoon sesame oil

3 scallions, finely diced (thoroughly washed and dried)

■Permit fish, marinated, to stand for about 2 hours at room
temperature. Place in crack-proof dish.

■Place 2 sets of chopsticks or a baking rack in wok, over
water. Water should not touch chopsticks or rack.

■Bring water to a boil and place dish with fish on the chopsticks or rack. (If fish is too large it may be cut in half, though
naturally and esthetically it should remain whole.) Cover the
wok and steam for ½ to ¾ hour, or until a chopstick can be
easily inserted into the fish flesh.

■Remove fish from wok and pour 2 tablespoons of boiled peanut oil over it. (The oil may be boiled a day in advance.
When oil boils, wisps of smoke can be seen.) It need not be
hot when poured over fish.

■Sprinkle diced scallions over fish and serve immediately.

Yield: 6 servings.

Won

Tons

Of infinite variety is the won ton. Once made it can be boiled, put into soup, pan-fried, deep-fat fried, or steamed. It can be an hors d'oeuvre, a first course, an ingredient in a larger scheme. And perhaps best of all, if it is left over it can be frozen to be enjoyed on another day. But first, here is the basic won ton:

In a large mixing bowl combine and stir clockwise:

1 pound fresh ground pork

½ pound shrimp (shelled, deveined, washed in salt water, drained, dried with a paper towel, and finely diced)

12 scallions (washed, dried thoroughly, both ends discarded, and finely chopped)

2 cloves garlic, minced

6 fresh water chestnuts (peeled, washed, dried, finely diced)

1 tablespoon white wine mixed with 1½ teaspoons ginger juice

1½ teaspoons salt

1½ teaspoons sugar

1½ teaspoons light soy sauce

1½ teaspoons sesame oil

1½ teaspoons oyster sauce

pinch of white pepper

3 to 4 tablespoons cornstarch

1 to 2 eggs (add last—they need not be beaten)

■Place about 1 tablespoon of above mixture in each skin of a 1-pound package of won ton skins. (Skins should be kept in plastic wrap at room temperature; then, 20 minutes before preparation, they should be peeled off and covered with a wet towel.)

■Keep a bowl of water at hand so that the four edges of the won ton skin can be wet. The meat should be placed on the non-floured side of the skin. Then the skin should be folded and squeezed along the wet edges to seal it like an envelope.

■Once folded and sealed, the 2 corners of the folded side are wetted and then drawn together and squeezed with the fingers to create a bow-like dumpling.

■Place each won ton on a floured cookie sheet.

■Cook the won tons in 3 quarts of boiling water to which 2 tablespoons of salt and 1 tablespoon of peanut oil have been added.

■Usual cooking time is 5 to 7 minutes, or until the filling can be seen through the skin.

■Remove pot of won tons from heat and run cold water into it. Drain off. Add more cold water running through the won tons. Place them on waxed paper and let them dry.

These can be eaten as they are, or they can be:

Pan-fried: Place 3 tablespoons of peanut oil in a flat pan, heat oil until a wisp of smoke can be seen. Place won tons in pan and fry until brown on both sides.

Deep-fat fried: Place 4 to 5 cups peanut oil in a wok. Boil the oil (oil boils when white smoke rises from it), add a slice of ginger and a clove of garlic and fry to a golden brown.

Put into soup: To 4 cups of chicken broth brought to a boil, add won tons—3 per person. Let the soup come to a boil again, then add 4 cups of shredded lettuce and serve.

Note: If freezing, make certain they are thoroughly dry. Double-wrap in plastic and then in foil.

Yield: 40 to 50 won tons

The Beggar's Chicken. The
legend is that a man stole a
chicken and, to cook it sur-
reptitiously, encased it in
clay and placed it next to hot
coals in a hole in the ground.

A Suzhou specialty. Beggar's Chicken is stuffed with pork, vegetables, and spices, and cooked for a long time in its clay housing. The waiter will strike it with a hammer to break the clay and liberate the food.